The Amazing Cigar

THE CIGAR CONNOISSEUR'S SECRETS TO SMOKE RINGS, MYSTIFICATIONS AND OTHER COOL THINGS

by

GIOVANNI LIVERA
JON RACHERBAUMER

Published by
MAGIC MARKETING CONCEPTS, INC.

Printed and Bound in the United States
First Edition
15 14 13 12 11 10 9 8 7 6 5 4 3 2 1

ISBN 0-9660567-2-8

Library of Congress Catalog Card Number: 97-76613

For Krys Livera and Jessica B Hack,
for understanding what lies beyond smoke and mirrors

ACKNOWLEDGEMENTS

Deepest thanks to Sue Adamczak, Alan James Novotny, Martin Gardner, Harry Garrison, Bert Pichel Jr., Jessica Hack, Ry Racherbaumer, Doug Conn, Terri Anderson, Michelle Livera, Luann Henken, Robert Livera, Bill Brack, John Unrue, Mike Maury and Blue Smoke Productions for their assistance, encouragement, and enthusiastic feedback.

Illustrated by Earle Oakes

Layout by Backbone Design
Character Artwork by Devin Crane

Special thanks to Bert Pichel, Jr. for use of photos from his collection

All photos of Giovanni by John Unrue,
except Aqua Rings shot by Bill Brack

CONTENTS

OLD BLACK MATCH-IK

MATCHBOX BAMBOOZLERS

MIND GAMES

INTRODUCTION

There is More to a Cigar...

Mystery is part of the world's bounty, waiting to be discovered, pointed out, and celebrated. Magicians remind us of this fact when they do extraordinary things with *ordinary* things. Being both magicians and cigar aficionados, we know the potential entertainment that often lies at our fingertips. We know the hypnotic attraction of blowing smoke rings. We know the "wow-factor" of levitating cigars, haunting matchboxes, and reading minds with ashes. We know there is more, *much more*, to cigars and their accouterments than anyone knows. And you, too, will discover that all kinds of amusing tomfoolery are possible—tricks, puzzles, and mysteries with common objects other than cigars: wrappers, bands, lighters, matches, matchboxes, cigar boxes, cigar ash, and—yes!—even *smoke!* We will explain the real secrets of blowing smoke rings!

Most of you know and savor the ceremonial rite of choosing, buying, and smoking a good cigar. Its popularity is a phenomenon; but we have always known that smoking cigars is a bonding ritual as ingratiating as the wraith-like smoke that fills the air. We know there is something warmly chummy about a room full of cigar aficionados. What many of you don't know is that the aromatic mist, like the mists imagined at Merlin's hideaway, is an ideal surrounding for *amazing* things to happen. When you are at your favorite cigar parlor, smoke-easy, or at a fellow smoker's home, you can do things that will suddenly turn heads, widen eyes, and make jaws drop. You will be able to make your friends say, "Wow! Do *that* again!"

Magicians, like cigar smokers, are drawn to intimate surroundings where everyone is relaxed and receptive. Moods are more mellow. These are ideal places to bring *The Amazing Cigar* to life. And the amazing, novel things we explain are (as the French say) perfect *divertissements* to show, share, and enjoy. Your friends, as well as you, will never look at cigars, smoke, cutters, lighters, and matches in a conventional way again. The late Lord Buckley, comic and commentator, called this combination of inspired fun-and-games "wig bubbles"—moments that effervesce in your mind; moments that make you laugh and say, "Wow!"

Enjoy,

Giovanni Livera

Jon Racherbaumer

HOW TO READ THIS BOOK

You can read and enjoy this book in one fell swoop, in small snack-like snatches (which is easier to do than to *say*), while on vacation, at the beach, during coffee breaks, or on a flight to Pago Pago. Unlike a novel, which must be read in sequence, this book is proudly bereft of order and grand design. It is an entertaining collection of diverse parts. Choose any chapter that strikes your fancy. Each trick, stunt, feat, or puzzle is self-contained, and each of the chapters is modular. They are all related and can be fitted together any way you like. This is part of the fun.

We have chosen material that is relatively easy to master, requiring props you are likely to have at your fingertips. Please note that the material is rated by the number of cigars that follow each item.

        = Easy

        = Moderately Easy

        = Challenging

        = For Those Eager To Reach New Levels

Most of the material can be understood and learned by *everyone*. However, we purposely included material for the *cognoscenti*—all the cigar-smokers who are discerning, aspiring, and eager to reach new levels of knowledge and expertise. We also sought diversity—everything from how to blow significantly different smoke rings to how to perform subtle mysteries using unusual and unexpected ingredients such as cigar ash. Remember: There is great pleasure in doing what people think cannot be done. And after reading this book, we are certain you will learn this firsthand.

Keep in mind that the explanations of these tricks are merely a framework. You, as a presenter, will make or break these tricks as you perform them for your fellow smokers. After you have mastered the steps required to make a given trick, stunt, or puzzle work, your task is to add *personality*. What you say and do and *how* you say and do it will enliven these explanations. Enjoy yourself. Have fun. If you have fun, your fellow smokers will enjoy themselves. Professional magicians live and die by this essential principle. Sometimes explanations seem uninteresting and mediocre, yet if you can sense how it will "play" in the real world, you will be ahead of the game. In short, try everything. Experiment. You will be happily surprised at the emotional power of these tricks. Practice them and *enjoy* practicing. Then try them out on your friends, colleagues, and fellow smokers. Each time you perform, you will become more proficient and this proficiency, coupled with the fun you provide, will stimulate you to continue entertaining. After all, it is fun. This is how most magicians are born, and why they never lose their child-heart and are always grinning. Join the club.

PRESENTATION TIPS

Leo Behnke, a professional magician and one of the first close-up performers to work the famous Magic Castle in Hollywood, California, writes: "Magic is a paradox—it is and it isn't. It can apparently suspend the laws of nature, but it needs the laws of science to succeed. A careless or sloppy performance will hurt a trick, but care and practice make magic as popular today as it ever was."

The tricks, stunts, and puzzles in this book have been audience-tested. Most people enjoy seeing novel and offbeat things. People love magical things. For "magic" to happen, as mentioned elsewhere in this book, largely depends on you. Here are some helpful hints that will make your presentations more successful and entertaining.

SURPRISE: This is a hallmark of magic, jokes, and film. Your ultimate goal is to surprise your friends. It will make them laugh. Therefore, never tell your friends exactly what you are going to do. Let your trick or stunt reveal itself gradually—or suddenly, if that what the trick calls for—as you lead them to an unexpected climax.

SIMPLICITY: Keep in mind the well-known KISS Principle, which is an acronym for Keep It Simple, Stupid! As you will discover while reading this book, many of the secrets to the tricks and puzzles are simple. The key to great magic is simplicity of method and simplicity of plot. Make certain that your audience grasps the plot, and then proceed in a direct manner. You, the person, can be as complicated as you like, but keep the rest simple.

REHEARSAL: Practice the tricks until you can perform them smoothly and without having to think about what comes next. The steps should become second nature so that you can concentrate on being yourself and expressing yourself in an amusing way. In turn, you will become supremely confident about what you are doing.

CREATE FUN: Many tricks and stunts are intrinsically funny and create an atmosphere of fun. If you are a good storyteller, add this element to your performances. If you know relevant jokes or suitable one-liners, add them to your repertoire.

Learning how to present these tricks, stunts and puzzles is a little like learning a second language. However, one of the beguiling aspects of learning what is in this book is that beginners will learn many cool things they can do right away. The key word is fun. If you are having a good time and want your friends to have fun, the rest is relatively easy. Turn the page and see for yourself.

SMOKE SORCERY

BERT PICHEL:
AN AMERICAN ORIGINAL

It probably started out innocently enough—a man in a garage enjoying a good cigar, feeling light-hearted, and expressing his elation by blowing smoke rings. The air was still, the hour was late, and no one was around. Then it happened: he blew a ring of such symmetry and duration that he was inspired to duplicate it. Naturally, he tried again and again and soon he was blowing better rings. And this inspired him to be playful and outrageous. Why not dozens of rings? Why not heart-shaped rings? Sometimes he surprised himself. Soon he would surprise and astonish *everybody*.

Twenty cigars a day produces lots of smoke, and soon his practice sessions resulted in an incredible repertoire. His smoke-ring-blowing virtuosity was about to become legend. Bert Pichel, a mild-mannered guy from Cincinnati, would soon become a specialized entertainer, exponent of advanced "fumiolatry," the art and love of blowing smoke rings.

Pichel, born in 1902, actually owned a gas station, a place with lots of daily social interaction and intermittent downtime. During this downtime, he smoked cigars. Lots of them. And he blew thousands of smoke rings and single-handedly revived the forgotten art of fumiolatry. Forget about the fashionable young men in the 16th century who performed exotic tricks in exhibitionistic ways. Forget about the Slights, Whiffle, Retention, Gulpe, or the infamous Cuban Ebolition! Bert Pichel, without benefit of counsel or instruction, invented new forms and took smoke-ring blowing to a level just north of the Far Side. He did things that Ripley could not believe, that were as strange as they seemed, and that were fantastic enough to be reported, praised, and televised worldwide. He was our first World Champion Smoke-Ring Blower and he remained unrivaled, unchallenged, and unbeaten during his lifetime.

Bert Pichel started smoking cigars and blowing smoke rings in 1922, and by the time newspapers and magazines started reporting his prowess, he had been blowing rings for at least 18 years. He once estimated that he smoked over 240,000 cigars and was always quoted as saying, "My lips are remarkably developed!"—a believable statement considering that on many occasions he blew up to 27 smoke rings on only *one* puff. Keep in mind that Pichel defined a *regulation* smoke ring as being at least three inches in diameter. He also holds a number of amazing records, the most impressive being that he once blew a ring so large it encircled a 46-inch weather balloon. He did everything with smoke rings except make them talk. Imagine blowing a figure-eight ring or passing a hat through a ring or blowing a ring from several feet so that it encircles a woman's delicately pointing toes! His grand finale, still unduplicated today, was to *simultaneously* blow *two rings* from a single puff.

Below is Pichel's own handwritten nightclub routine.

Routine :-

(1.) Blow a simple Smoke Ring!

(2) Blow a ring thru a Ring!

(3) Blow a ring and turn it over!

(4) Shrink a Ring

(5) Blow two rings

(6.) Push hat thru.

— Announcer —

(7) Ring over Packs of Cigarettes!

(8) Ring up to Halo!

Bert Pichel was an American original who created a second, unusual career and became an international sensation. Fortunately, his mantle and knowledge were passed onto Harry Garrison, who not only carries on this fascinating and esoteric tradition, but has added to it... .

HARRY GARRISON:
LORD OF THE RINGS

He looks like he stepped out of a book by Dickens. His bearing bespeaks another time, another place. There is something serene and magisterial in his voice, yet he seems comfortably at home wherever he is—a duke in his domain, as he casually talks and leisurely walks. But his stroll is not exactly casual. If you watch closely, you see what it really is—a subtle reconnaissance. He is checking out the room—its capacity and atmospherics, its interior weather. The room, you see, is the physical medium of his art. And the very air, by God, must be perfectly still and mute as a golden dawn. *"This,"* he drolly notes with a wave of his hand, *"is the smoke-ring blowing arena."* That having been said, Harry Garrison surveys the crowd and flicks the end of his cigar.

"This is one of the few performances," he intones, *"where the cigar gets stronger and the performer gets weaker."*

He takes a couple of preliminary puffs. They are not ordinary puffs, but are taken in with focused resolve. It reminds you of the way baseball pitchers stylishly wind up to throw. It expresses the same kind of concentration. He eventually holds in a mouthful of smoke, leans outward, places a flattened hand next to his cheek, and suddenly bobs his head a bit. A perfect orb of smoke rolls from his lips, glides forward, and forms an immaculate, tremulous O. It slowly loses momentum and while still gliding, expands and levitates in a delicate, disembodied way. Garrison has begun.

"A simple, introductory ring!" he booms. He puffs, conjures another, and deftly moves behind it with little cat steps. He stops short, places a flat hand an inch behind the ring, gently pushes against the air between it and the wondrous O, and nudges it in any direction he wants it to go. And go it does, rolling outward, still expanding—a sudden conjuration that turns the room into a church. The crowd gazes at the center of the widening O as it evolves and dilates into the distance. Garrison watches as well, delighted by the ring's felicitous passage into space and eventual nothingness. Everyone wants to say something about what they have seen, but they remain silent until Garrison comments: *"A gently wafting ring..."* He pauses and adds with utter seriousness, *"I want to thank you for your indulgent compliance to my cautionary remarks regarding the constant flailing about of arms and hands...It discombobulates the air in the smoke-ring blowing arena."* The audience laughs.

Harry Garrison is a world-class smoke ringer and the only true successor and promoter of the same smoke-ring blowing artistry made famous by Bert Pichel. But "blower" does not define what he does or how he does it. The physics seems straightforward enough. He controls air and creates *visible vortices of smoke.* He can also determine their size, shape, and fate. And when he does, an idle pastime is raised to a higher level. Sometimes a spectator mistakes the weightiness of Garrison's lofty approach and dares to titter. He is quickly admonished. *"This is serious,"* Garrison facetiously scolds. *"It is not a comedic turn."*

Garrison then proceeds to dominate the smoke-ring blowing arena, offering pontifications, casual asides, and bits of arcane trivia. Throughout his rambling discourse, he blows small rings, big rings, rings-within-rings, streams of miniature rings, leapfrog rings, and rings with *character!* *"In the past,"* he adds, *"I took delicate pleasure in naming every ring, pointing out subtle differences... . There are many varieties. There is the steadfast ring; the gently wafting ring; the explosive, soaring ring; the slightly dissipated ring; and so on... ."*

He stops from time to time for some libation. *"In recent years,"* he says, *"doctors have advised me to counter the toxicity of the nicotine poisoning with strong bourbon-whiskey or cognac, when it is available, to remoisturize the inner mucosa of the upper pharyngeal cavity to permit the continuance of the performance."* He takes a few measured sips, then turns to the crowd and blows a perfectly aimed ring that glides like a bride down a church aisle. As it grows and grows, Garrison's voice becomes fuller.

"A grand smoke ring..."
As the ring expands to the size of a hula hoop, he adds, *"...a ring of true greatness...a ring of lasting majesty...there...in the atmosphere!"*
He blows another and by using his flat hand, he gradually turns the ring and directs it to the ceiling. *"A ceiling ring,"* he muses, *"sent skyward for the gods*

and those in the leeward seats." He propels another, then blows on it and makes it instantly disappear. He grins. *"The vanishing ring... ."*

He speaks with reverence about his mentor. *"The previous world-champion smoke ring blower, Bertram Pichel...P-I-C-H-E-L...one day knocked on my front door with a newspaper clipping in his hand. He was infuriated that an Englishman was claiming that he could blow a hundred and eight smoke rings in a row. 'Those aren't smoke rings,' he shouted. 'Those are ringlets!' And he was right. Ringlets are not bona fide rings. I will show you the difference."*

The difference is likened to the voiced and unvoiced sounds of the vocal cords. Garrison makes the two different sounds, takes a puff on his cigar, and emits a stream of small, concentric smoke rings, accompanied by the proper phonetic sound. *"Ringlets,"* he scoffs, *"are made by unvoiced sounds and little coughs... Pathetic!"* Then, standing as erect as a general, he blows a perfect ring, followed by another, faster-moving ring that glides through the center of the first ring. *"Those,"* he adds, *"are real rings of an infinitely different pedigree! I once called them Perfecto!"*

The audience is mute. They have surrendered. They believe. Garrison has amused, edified, and converted them. They will now believe *anything* he says, even when he says, *"There are only 14,000 of us. Our annual meeting is held at the Princess Hotel in Acapulco. We publish the Smoke-Ring Blower's Almanac, which once a year publishes the annual challenge...."* It does not matter. Fact and fiction merge. Everyone now imagines a convention of ring blowers and ring-masters. The air is misty with smoke. They see them sitting around, laughing, cutting up, and blowing incredible smoke rings. The image adheres. And when Garrison ends his performance and thanks the audience for their kind attention, he toasts them by taking a last sip of cognac from his glass. The faces of the crowd look satisfied, beatific. They are content, perhaps as content as smokers, puffing a great cigar, are content. But rest assured, they will remember what they have seen today. They will remember Garrison, purveyor of fanciful, beguiling, disappearing smoke rings. Like the artifacts of dreamers, dreaming, they will remember the indelible image of a giant ring of whitish smoke, levitating in the dark for an instant in time, a testament to both beauty and impermanence and perhaps man's place in the same domain.

You can also learn to be a champion smoke-ring blower.
Read on...

RING MASTERY

Learning how to blow smoke rings is part of a smoker's rite of passage. It tacitly expresses one's mastery over the entire ritual of lighting a cigar, taking in smoke, savoring its taste, smelling its aroma, then exhaling it in a novel, carefree, and—to use an unusual word!—*ebullient* manner. Yes, exhalations shaped in the roundness of "rings" are artful, *visible* ebullitions. They appear suddenly, moving outward from O-shaped mouths, rolling, expanding, and widening, propelled by a vortex of mute pleasure. They are momentarily hypnotic. The exhaler looks thoughtful, a person in control. Instead of a defeatist's sigh, the smoke ring is more like a lover's swoon, signaling that everything is right with the world in this instant; that everything is cool and wonderful.

THE SMOKE

Cigar smoke is thicker than cigarette smoke, and this thickness differs with various types of cigars. Wait until your cigar has been smoking for awhile and you have taken about eight puffs. Once it is "broken in" and smoke can be evenly drawn, draw in a substantial amount of smoke and completely fill your mouth. Try to keep most of the smoke toward the back of your mouth.

MOUTH POSITIONS

There are two basic positions: (1) The pucker; (2) The enfolded lips. The pucker consists of pursing your lips into an O-shape. The enfolded technique consists of opening your mouth and drawing your lips inward against your upper and lower teeth.

(1) The pucker

(2) The enfolded lips

The opening formed by your lips can be adjusted to various sizes like the aperture of a camera. The size of the opening determines the *initial* size of the smoke ring as it comes out through this opening.

PROPULSION

Giovanni performs the Coughing Technique

There are four basic ways to propel accumulated smoke through the opening formed by your lips. The two most common propelling techniques use a cough or your tongue. Bert Pichel used the coughing technique and Harry Garrison still does.

The Coughing Technique: The objective is to use the inside of your mouth as the smoke-chamber, then emit air behind the smoke gathered at the opening of your lips with a cough. The resultant burst of air will push out the smoke and form the necessary vortex and subsequent smoke ring.

The Tongue Technique: This is done by resting the tip of your tongue at the bottom of your lower, inner gum. Anchor it there as the rest of your tongue retracts in preparation to thrust forward.

The top of your tongue moves outward and toward your lips. The smoke situated in front of it will be propelled outward when you thrust it forward. You will also exhale some air. This slight, perfectly modulated exhalation, when it is coupled with the outward thrust of your tongue, propels the smoke through your O-shaped lips.

These two coordinated actions form a vortex and the result will be a ring of smoke that moves outward in the direction of its propulsion.

Jaw Technique: Moving your jaw can also act like a bellows, causing air to surge outwards through your lips.

Tap Technique: The other form of propulsion is the tap, which is used to form ringlets. (See "Ringlets")

As mentioned earlier, the size of the ring depends on the size of your O-shaped lips. The speed of the smoke ring's outward propulsion depends on the degree of tongue thrusting and exhalation. Usually there is enough smoke in your mouth to blow three or four rings in quick succession. As mentioned earlier, the father of smoke rings, Bert Pichel, could blow 27 three-inch rings on one puff. If you prefer, without altering the basic O-shape, you can increase the size of your smoke rings by pulling your upper lip against your upper teeth and slightly dropping your lower jaw. The diameter of the O-shape should be about an inch.

Concentrate on gently *pushing* out the smoke. It is not so much blown out as it is facilitated by a delicate, coordinated act. For some, the tongue is the best facilitator. But if you want to emulate the champions, develop the cough-propulsion technique.

PRACTICE

There are four things to practice: (1) Controlling the volume of smoke you can accommodate in your mouth or "holding chamber;" (2) modulating the surge of smoke as the vortex is created; (3) modulating the initial sizes of the rings; and (4) controlling the direction of the ring's glide path and striving for calculated accuracy. Pichel hung embroidery hoops to the ceiling with thread for practice. He would then stand back at different distances and aim smoke rings at the hoops.

AIR CURRENTS

A critical aspect to keep in mind is air currents. Ruffled air, vagrant breezes, and air-conditioned currents are your enemy. Anything that discombobulates the air will effect the delicate vortex of smoke rings. Smoke rings can be created outdoors, but the life of such a ring is abruptly cut short and the quality is inferior. While Pichel got his start and practiced in garages and basements, the best atmosphere is a *still* drawing room, lined with books, furnished in wood and leather, and lit by candles. Everyone in the room should refrain from talking. Shouting and sighing cannot be permitted. Deflected whispers are allowed, but discouraged. Smoke rings love *dead air*. Create them in serenity and silence and in hallowed places where they can languidly glide and gradually dissipate.

Yes, vagrant air currents are the enemy of smoke ringers. Harry Garrison, made an amusing appearance on *The Tonight Show with Johnny Carson* (which became part of Carson's all-time blooper collection) in which the air-conditioning drafts thwarted Garrison's attempts to sustain any rings. The same thing happened to Pichel when he appeared on a television show called *Club 49.* He was introduced, his theme music—"Smoke Gets In Your Eyes"—started playing and he began to blow. The first few rings were perfect, but when gusts of air interfered, his rings began to dissipate and, as a newspaper reviewer put it, "things went up in smoke." When Pichel tried to end with his Halo Trick, he turned to the female host and said, "You are an angel and if you will look into your mirror, you will see a halo around your head." The host pulled out her compact and started looking in the mirror. Pichel started puffing and blowing like a madman and soon the host was enveloped in a smoke screen. No halo appeared, and when she suddenly emerged, coughing and sputtering, the band played a rendition of "Dixie." That's show business!

DRAFTING

This technique was perfected by Pichel and passed onto Garrison, who uses it with authority and expertise.

HOW IT WORKS

Once a smoke ring has been blown and slows to its moderate cruising speed, place a flat hand about an inch behind it. Push against the air space immediately behind the ring. This results in propelling the ring faster in the direction of this nudging push. If you tilt your fingertips backward, the pressure of the "pushed" air becomes uneven. The heel of your hand exerts more influence and the lowermost air is more powerful. Consequently, the aerodynamics of the ring is affected and the ring itself will turn on its vertical axis. It will tilt backwards. By continuing to turn your flat hand, you can gradually alter the flight path of the ring.

Pichel expertly demonstrates drafting in this vintage photo.

18

You can cause the ring, for example, to move in a vertical path or turn to the left, right, or move directly downward. This omni-directional facility must be delicately performed while the integrity of the ring still remains. Keep in mind that the life span of a smoke ring is short, measured in seconds. If the air is completely still, some rings may last 30-45 seconds, growing to 20-30 inches in diameter. Act fast.

AMAZING CIGAR FACTOID

The smallest commercially produced cigar was the Bolivar Delgado, which measured less than 1.5 inches long.

RINGLETS

It is possible to generate dozens of small smoke rings from a single mouthful of smoke. In fact, if your friends don't know this, you can win many bets.

HOW IT WORKS The initial dynamics follow "Ring Mastery." Draw in a substantial amount of smoke and completely fill your mouth. Try to keep most of the smoke toward the back of your mouth.

This time, your tongue does not play a major part. Rest the tip of your tongue at the bottom of your lower, inner gum and anchor it there. The rest of your tongue retracts as your lips purse into a *tiny* O-shape. The smoke rings are emitted from this itty-bitty opening.

The means of propulsion consists of gently but sharply *tapping* one of your cheeks with a forefinger. Do this repeatedly until at least twenty tiny rings are propelled into the air. You can also do this, as Garrison suggests, by emitting tiny, successive *small coughs* from your pharyngeal cavity.

Mouth position for Ringlets. You may look goofy, but the end result is worth it!

You will be amazed at how many rings can be formed in this manner. The more rapidly you flick, the shorter the distance between the individual rings that will move out in a steady stream.

Giovanni demonstrates Ringlets.

The same stunt has been done using a cigarette pack—say, a pack of Camels. All the cigarettes are removed and a toothpick or pin is used to puncture a hole in the side of the pack. This hole is made where the camel's mouth would be. Then the inside of the pack is filled with cigarette or cigar smoke, which is simply exhaled through the opening at the top used to access the cigarettes. The operator's hand covers the top opening to prevent the smoke from escaping. All that remains is to gently tap the side of the pack with a finger. Each tap causes an itty-bitty smoke ring to come out of the camel's mouth.

HOLE-IN-ONE

This special feat was devised by Pichel and is currently performed by Garrison. After you have mastered the art of blowing *basic* smoke rings and can dispatch them with easy abandon, you will be ready to try advanced feats.

HOW IT WORKS

You release and send a smoke ring airborne, then immediately send another ring, speedier than the first, which passes through the first one. As they pass, the first ring slows and expands. This is repeated with another ring, followed by another ring, until all dissipate.

The critical aspect is to be able to accurately direct the smoke rings you propel into the air. Not only is the direction important, but the relative speed of the rings plays an important part.

20

Pichel performs Hole-In-One.

Send the initial ring forward at regular speed. As soon as it expands to about two inches in diameter, aim and propel another ring toward the center of the first ring. This ring is propelled at a much faster velocity.

Most of the time the second ring simply passes through the first one. However, if the relative forward speed of both rings is just right, when the second ring passes through the first one, the first one will contract and speed up and the second ring will expand and slow down. If you do not blow another ring, the back-and-forth activity of the two rings will continue until the smoke thins and dissipates. When this happens, it is a joy to behold.

Garrison often blows three or four rings in a row, each one gliding through the preceding ones. Also practice blowing two rings through one, three rings through two, and four through three rings. These stunts are great for practicing aim and velocity.

FIGURE EIGHTS

HOW IT WORKS

Blow a ring downward and onto a table. Quickly blow another ring on top of the first. Both rings will momentarily merge for a split second, then will form a figure eight. If you can do this stunt, you are ready to compete on the expert level.

The Figure Eight blown by Pichel.

OFF THE WALL

HOW IT WORKS

You can also propel a single ring at above-average speed toward an expansive flat surface such as a wall. When it gets close to the wall, the ring will dramatically expand. The physics that explains this phenomenon has to do with the dynamics of airflow. The perpendicular airflow caused by the *opposite* perpendicular airflow striking the solidity of the wall and bouncing back causes the ring to expand. It is also interesting to try this stunt against a mirror.

NOTHING TO BE SNIFFED AT

The only smoke ringer known to have mastered this stunt is Pichel.

HOW IT WORKS
Blow a ring outward at moderate velocity, then move close enough to the ring with your nose so that you can sniff part of the ring back into the "holding chamber." This, correctly done, will cut the initial ring in half.

Without too much hesitation, expel the "sniffed back" smoke as another full-bodied ring. This form of recycling requires a strong constitution, lots of practice, and the right circumstances. Sneezing, needless to say, creates a completely different outcome.

DISAPPEARING RING

Garrison uses it as a sight gag. After the ring disappears, he states the obvious: *"The disappearing ring!"* It usually gets a laugh.

HOW IT WORKS
After you have formed a ring, slowly sneak up behind it and blow a steady, narrow stream of air at its center. This causes a vacuum. The ring will then rapidly contract into nothingness. Do not underestimate this stunt. It must be seen to be appreciated.

MERGER

This stunt sounds impossible, but Pichel actually performed it.

HOW IT WORKS The ringer blows a single ring and when it slows, he blows a stream of smoke that hits a section of the established ring and is absorbed. You literally blow smoke into another ring.

There is not any elaborate technique except to do it. It is strictly a matter of practice and experimentation. The second stream of smoke, however, must hit the first ring at the right velocity. Sometimes you can move your mouth right next to the ring and release the second stream of smoke into the vortex.

In some instances, it is possible to *link* two rings. This is also a matter of delicate timing. Pichel was adept at performing this stunt.

HAT TRICK

Pichel demonstrates the Hat Trick with ease.

HOW IT WORKS Blow a standard ring at moderate speed so that it is in front of your body about chest level. Hold the top of your hat in your right hand with the brim and head opening toward the ring. Move the hat toward the ring. (Photo 1)

Because the hat is much larger than your hand, the drafting principle works beautifully. The ring will slowly and inevitably widen. When it expands wider than the circumference of your hat's brim, gingerly push the hat through the ring. (Photo 2)

(Photo 1)

(Photo 2)

PICHEL'S HALO

HOW
IT WORKS

You must create a robust smoke ring that is blown so that the ring is parallel with the ceiling and slows to a point of suspension at eye-level. While more or less hovering in this state, it must also widen enough for your head to duck underneath. You can then wear it as a temporary halo.

DOUBLE RING ✦✦✦✦ +

This may be the most remarkable stunt from Pichel's repertoire. We have seen only the amazing *results* in photographs and on film. As far as we know, Pichel was the only ringer to master this incredible stunt.

HOW
(WE THINK)
IT WORKS

It seems logical that your lips must somehow be partitioned as to expel smoke in two different directions while *simultaneously* forming two, distinct vortices. Pichel used the cigar, in part, as a partition. He took in some smoke and placed the cigar in the center of his mouth, then he blew or coughed out two rings.

Good luck.

24

AQUA RINGS

Comic artist George Storm created a character named Colonel Porterhouse, who could smoke cigars under water. This may or may not have inspired Ernie Kovacs, a great comedian and cigar smoker, to emulate this wild and crazy stunt. Like Storm and Kovacs, Giovanni, believe it or not, blows smoke rings underwater! He got the idea when he was learning to scuba dive and his instructor, Bill Brack, showed him an air-bubble vortex. That is, he tilted his head backwards while twenty feet under water, removed his regulator from his mouth, and released a bubble-ring that rose to the surface.

HOW IT WORKS

Giovanni discovered that you can have someone hand you a cigar at the deep end of a swimming pool. You then take in a mouthful of thick smoke and submerge yourself a minimum of two to three feet. Wearing an underwater mask prevents air from escaping through your nose as well as giving you a clear view of your creation. Tilt your head back so that the surface of your mouth is parallel with the surface of the water. Pucker your lips and release the smoke by saying, *"Pwop!"* The explosive action of blowing out this word and cutting it off in mid-P will release a *smoky* bubble-ring. It will rise to the surface and when it breaks through, the smoke ring becomes airborne.

Giovanni lying down at the bottom of a pool blowing Aqua Rings.

This stunt demands a zany streak of adventuresomeness. As Giovanni puts it, it only works when the air is still, the water is calm, and the planets are aligned. When it does, it is a beautiful thing. It's best to practice the ring bubble before adding smoke to your mouth. The best vantage point for spectators to watch is from the diving board with the performer submerged below.

25

MOOD RINGS

Once you have mastered blowing a standard ring, you can experiment with theatrical and colorful ways to add personality and emotion to the ring itself. This is done by facial expressions, body language, and attitude. The following list will give you some ideas.

Contemplative: Close your eyes and place your fingertips at your temples, then blow a ring upward.

Competitive: Blow rings through *someone else's* rings.

Affluent: Celebratory rings after the major deal.

Shy: Blow rings in a darkened closet or with your jacket pulled over your head.

Jock: Crouch and bend over as though you were a football center, then blow a ring through your legs.

Self-destructive: Blow rings into a whirling fan.

Defiant: Blow a smoke ring into your opponent's face followed by the rest of the smoke in your mouth.

Outlaw: Blow rings from a smoking section into a non-smoking section.

Optimistic: Blow rings outdoors in Chicago.

Extreme Optimist: Blow rings outdoors in Chicago during a rainstorm.

Vulgar: Blow a ring while simultaneously belching.

Zen: Blow rings without a cigar.

Polar Rings: Blow a ring in below-zero temperatures with your cold breath.

Carefree: Blow rings completely naked.

Stupid: Blow polar rings completely naked.

Frat-House: Blow rings and pretend to eat them.

Bravado: Usually done in a standing position with the attitude that you own the room. The ring of confidence.

Vicarious: Talk about other smoker's rings.

Seductive: Look directly into your desired's eyes and blow one small ring to the side while focusing on your alluring lip movement.

MISTOLOGIST

Try this the next time you are a host-bartender. It does not take long for every-one to try pouring smoke from glass to glass.

WHAT YOU SEE
You ask the bartender for a couple of clean glasses. You take a couple of robust drags on your favorite cigar, pick up one of the glasses, and place it next to your lips. Smoke begins to languidly swirl and fill the glass. The glass is placed on the table for a few seconds as everyone watches the thick smoke swirl and settle into the glass. You then pick up the smoke-filled glass and slowly pour the smoke into the other glass. *"Yes,"* you proudly add, *"this is why I keep my day job!"* Then pick up the glass and proceed to drink the smoke.

WHAT YOU NEED
(1) A cigar. (2) Two empty glasses. Make sure that the glasses are cool and slightly moist inside. This is not absolutely necessary, but it makes the stunt work better.

HOW IT WORKS
Light your cigar and get it stoking. You should be in a place where the air is *absolutely still*. There cannot be any vagrant drafts, ruffled air, or gusts from a fan or air-conditioner. Ask onlookers to be silent. No talking.

Place an upright glass in your right hand and put the cigar in your mouth. Suck in deeply to get a mouthful of thick smoke. Hold the lip of the glass against your mouth so that your lower lip is on the out-side. Your mouth is open wide enough to permit smoke to *flow* out. (Fig. 1)

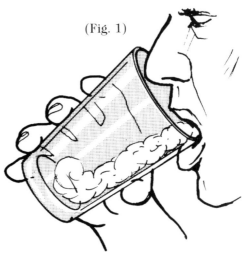

(Fig. 1)

Do not *blow* smoke outward. Gently ease the smoke out so that it flows out and *downward* into the glass. Any exhalation should be very, very faint. The smoke should swirl and settle as though it were magical syrup.

27

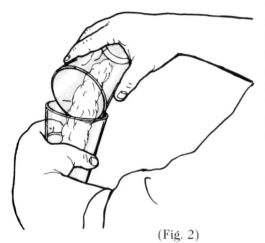

(Fig. 2)

The smoke will eventually settle near the bottom of the glass, forming a few layers in its protective, enclosed environment. After the smoke has settled and can be displayed for everyone to see, pick up the other upright glass with your left hand. If you cup a hand over the mouth of the glass, it has a stabilizing, settling effect.

Slowly and deliberately tilt the smoke-filled glass to a normal pouring position. Now the smoke will slowly "pour" from one glass to the other. (Fig. 2) Hold the glasses steady and let gravity do the rest. After several seconds, the smoke will settle into the left-hand glass. For the finale, lift the glass to your mouth and pretend to drink the smoke.

AMAZING CIGAR
QUOTE

"A man's shoes will tell you if he has money, his clothes if he has style. But if you want to know if he's a sport, see if he's wearing a good cigar."

—*Nat Sharman*

JP YOUR SLEEVE

his wacky stunt may be worth the extra trouble and preparation. It depends on
ie limits of your willingness to perform a strange stunt. Magician Arnold Belais
ıtroduced this trick at a convention for magicians and everybody loved it.

HAT YOU EE

You are gathered with a group of smokers and you suddenly take a
mouthful of smoke and apparently blow it up your sleeve. Much to
everyone's surprise, the smoke comes out of your *other* sleeve!

HAT YOU EED

(1) You need a length of rubber or plastic tubing about a quarter of an
inch in diameter. A convenient source is a pet store that sells plastic
tubing for aquariums. It must be long enough to go from the opening of
one sleeve, across the back of your jacket, to the other sleeve. (2) A
mouthpiece from a cigarette holder which can fit into one end of the
tube. (3) Two heavy-duty rubber bands or wrist guards. (4) A lit cigar.

OW WORKS

Anchor the ends of the tubes to your wrists with the mouthpiece end in
your right sleeve. The rest of the tube spans across your back to your
left sleeve. The mouthpiece must rest about an inch from the outside
edge of your sleeve. Slip on your coat and you are reasonably unen-
cumbered until you are ready to perform.

old your cigar in your left hand and say, *"I just thought of a weird way to redi-
:ct second-hand smoke."*

ıke a deep drag on your cigar
ıd raise your right hand to
ıe side of your face. Raise it
ıgh enough for your mouth to
ıove into the sleeve to contact
ıe mouthpiece of the tubing.
'ig. 1) The sleeve and your
ınd provide cover. It should
»ok like you are blowing
ınoke up your sleeve, when, in
:ality, you are exhaling smoke
ıto the tube. Raise your left
m and hand, pointing to the
ınaginary smoking section.

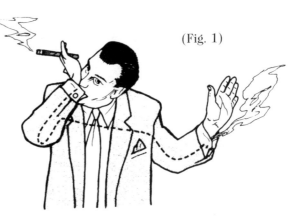

(Fig. 1)

l the preparation is worth it when you hear the laughing and watch the faces
your incredulous smoking partners.

SMUBBLES

A Smubble is smoke inside a soap bubble. Although he did not invent them, th
bubble-artistry of Tom Noddy made the public aware of them.

WHAT YOU SEE

Someone (probably a bubble-maker) said that a bubble is like desire
impossible to fully describe, yet everyone knows how it *feels*. It is won
der made round, wonder made full. Like snowflakes and human souls
no two bubbles are alike. They are incredibly delicate, translucen
globes that last long enough—just long enough—to be admired; an
when you introduce smoke inside their rounded skin, they have milk
opacity. They have heft and seeming solidity; when they pop and van
ish, the smoke remains longer, swirling in the wake of what used to be
The smoke is the aftermath to accompany the "wow" we want to utte
instead of squealing.

WHAT YOU NEED

(1) Bubble Soap. There are commercial solutions on the market, bu
you can make your own by combining dishwashing liquid such as Jo
with water and glycerin. Add fifteen parts water to one part dishwash
ing liquid. Add a few drops of glycerin to give the bubbles greate
longevity and tensile strength. (2) A plastic straw. (3) A lit cigar.

HOW IT WORKS

Dip an end of the plastic straw into the soap solution and hold it in on
hand. Draw in a mouthful of cigar smoke and blow the smoke into th
straw. The bubble will form and fill with smoke. (Photo 1)

(Photo 1)

(Photo 2)

Remove the straw from your mouth and dislodge the bubble with a small, sharp flick of your wrist. The bubble should float away in front of you. (Photo 2) You can direct its flight path by gently blowing in the direction you want it to go or by pushing a flat palm behind it.

For a cool effect, pop the bubble. (Photo 3)

(Photo 3)

FINGER SMOKE

This is a bit sophomoric, but try it when conversation turns to politics.

WHAT YOU SEE You are sitting around a table with friends, smoking your favorite cigar. You pick up a saltshaker and sprinkle some salt on your cigar, then you pick up the peppershaker and put some pepper on your right thumb and forefinger. You say, *"This stuff is hotter than you think."* You rub your thumb and forefinger together, ostensibly to generate a little more heat. *"Cavemen used to rub two sticks together to produce the same thing..."* Soon a column of smoke rises from your fingers.

A book of paper matches.

Remove the striking surface from a book of matches and place it in a ashtray. Light a match and burn this striking surface. It will eventually burn out, leaving a sticky residue and some ashes. Move the ashes away and brush your right thumb and forefinger against the residue. Th gunk will produce the "smoke."

Rub your prepared thumb and forefinger together. Keep doing this until they produce smoke-like fumes that rise from your thumb and fingers.

AUTO-SMOKE

Here's one to try your hand at.

As you are puffing on your favorite cigar, you say to your smokir buddy: *"I'll betcha this cigar can smoke itself!"* When your buddy giv you a blank look, you proceed to prove your claim.

A lit cigar.

Hold the lit cigar between your clasped hands so that the lit end protrudes from the thumb-side.

Do not clasp your fingers, but place your right fingers over the topside of you left hand. Your left fingers curl around your right hand. There is enough spac inside your hands to create a partial vacuum if your initial clasp is as airtight a possible.

Squeeze your palms together to form a slight vacuum, then relax them. Repea this "pumping" action several times and the cigar will chug and "smoke" itsel Your buddy will either grin or recommend that you need to get out more often

HOW MUCH DOES SMOKE WEIGH?

Giovanni took a healthy drag on his cigar, then blew a stream of smoke toward the ceiling, grinned, and asked, *"How much do you think the smoke in this cigar weighs?"*

Racherbaumer ignored him.

"No, I'm serious. How much do you think it weighs?"

Racherbaumer pondered the question. *"It weighs as much as the fizz in this tonic water...plus or minus, say...an ounce!"*

Giovanni took another puff and added, *"You don't know, do you? You really don't know!"*

"Do I need to know?"

"Yes, you need to know. Every cigar smoker needs to know."

"So tell me."

"First, you weigh the cigar without its wrapper and write down its weight. Then you cut off its end and save it. You smoke the cigar and save the ashes and the butt. You then weigh the ashes, the butt, and the cut-off end. Write down the total. Now subtract this sum from the total weight of the cigar before you smoked it. The result is how much the smoke weighs!"

"Like I said, why do I need to know this?"

"As they say about Mount Everest," chimed Giovanni, *"because it's there, buddy...because it's there!"*

33

CIGAR CHICANERY

Giovanni: "*Cigar smokers love to discuss tobacco horticulture and the various brands and prices. They know a lot about cutting, lighting, tapping, re-lighting, and puffing on them, but this section shows how to create real conversation pieces.*"

Racherbaumer: "*Yeah. A levitating cigar always raises eyebrows. Two in the hand beats a butt in the bush. Show me 'Close, But No Cigar' again! I love wagers you cannot lose.*"

HANG TIME

Illusionists have been floating ladies for eons. This is a mini-version with a cigar

WHAT YOU SEE   A cigar is held in a closed fist. When your hand is opened and held flat, the cigar remains suspended.

WHAT YOU NEED   (1) A cigar (a Churchill works best). (2) A good index finger.

HOW IT WORKS   Like many good stunts, its method is simple yet devious. Hold your favorite cigar in your left fist so that the cigar is perpendicular to the floor. Narrow, extra long cigars are perfect.

Turn your body to the right so that your left side is toward your fellow smokers. Grasp your left wrist with your right hand by placing your thumb on top and your second, third, and fourth fingers around the underside of your left wrist. Your right forefinger extends and remains hidden behind your fist. (Fig. 1)

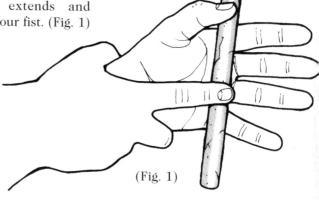

(Fig. 1)

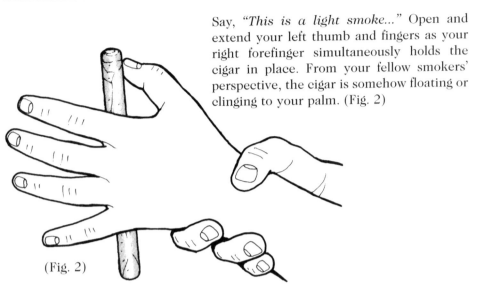

Say, *"This is a light smoke..."* Open and extend your left thumb and fingers as your right forefinger simultaneously holds the cigar in place. From your fellow smokers' perspective, the cigar is somehow floating or clinging to your palm. (Fig. 2)

(Fig. 2)

Continue: *"...very light...lighter than air."* Move both hands up and down, proving that the cigar is somehow clinging.

Close your left fingers around the cigar, then separate your hands and hand out the cigar for examination.

SUCKER'S HANG TIME

This is identical to "Hang Time," except it will fool the wise ones.

WHAT YOU SEE	A cigar is held in a closed fist. When your hand is opened and held flat, the cigar remains suspended. This time, your other hand stops holding the hand covering the suspended cigar.
WHAT YOU NEED	(1) A cigar. (2) A wristwatch. If you are not a watch-wearer, then encircle your wrist with a strong rubber band. (3) A pen or pencil. (A table knife also works in a pinch.)
HOW IT WORKS	This method is also simple, but is much more devious.

Insert the pen under your wristwatch so that one of the ends extends to the center of your left palm. You can hold your hand relaxed and in any state as long as you keep the back of your hand facing the spectator.

Hold your favorite cigar in your left fist so that the cigar is perpendicular to the floor, but it must also be between the pen and your palm, more or less wedged in place. (Fig. 1) Use a narrow, extra long cigar.

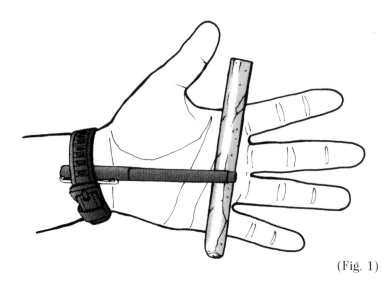

(Fig. 1)

Turn your body to the right so that your left side is toward your fellow smokers. Grasp your left wrist with your right hand by placing your thumb on top and your second, third, and fourth fingers around the underside of your left wrist. Your right forefinger extends and remains hidden behind your fist. This simulates the method used in "Hang Time."

Say, *"This is a light smoke..."* Open and extend your left thumb and fingers as your right forefinger simultaneously holds the cigar in place. From your fellow smokers' vantage point, the cigar is somehow floating or clinging to your palm. Continue: *"...very light...lighter than air."*

At this stage, anyone familiar with "Hang Time" will be nodding their heads and grinning. Move both hands up and down, proving that the cigar is somehow clinging to your flat palm. Now for the fun part. Move your right hand away from your left wrist and wave it over the top of the cigar, saying, *"Look! No hands!"* The cigar remains suspended.

Close your left fingers around the cigar, then pull the cigar free of the pen with your right hand, and then hand over the cigar for examination. You can remove the pen from your watchband at an opportune moment.

KLINGON

This is a quickie that can be used in conjunction with the other suspension stunts.

WHAT YOU SEE You are apparently able to keep a cigar upright and in temporary suspension without visible support. The cigar appears to be magnetized.

WHAT YOU NEED (1) A cigar. (2) A short straight pin.

HOW IT WORKS Push the straight pin into the middle of the cigar about a quarter of the way from the head. Because the pin has a small head on it, it is easily retracted.

Secretly pull out the pin halfway, then extend your left forefinger as though you were pointing. Place the cigar against the middle of your pointing forefinger with your right hand so that the retracted shaft of the pin rests on top. (Fig. 1)

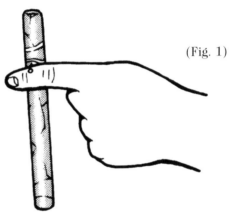

(Fig. 1)

The cigar will balance in place and you can remove your right hand. From your fellow smokers' point of view, the cigar looks magnetized or somehow suspended without visible means of support.

AMAZING CIGAR FACTOID

Several cigars have claimed over the years to being the largest cigar. The longest is probably the 50-inch monstrosity kept in the Partagas factory in Havana, but the Davidoff store in London displays a cigar that measures a yard in length with a whopping ring size of 96. (Ring size is diameter measured in sixty-fourths of an inch.)

PRAYER SUSPENSION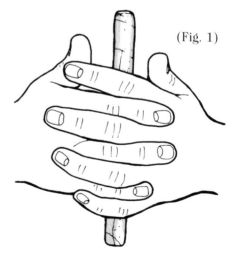

This is good for convincing your friends that your macrobiotic diet and yoga lessons have not been wasted.

WHAT YOU SEE You hold a cigar within clasped hands and then flatten your interlaced fingers. The cigar, without visible means of support, stays suspended or magnetized. On command, the cigar falls to the table.

WHAT YOU NEED A cigar.

HOW IT WORKS This requires a little practice getting your fingers coordinated. Begin by holding a cigar in a vertical position or upright in your left hand. The shaft of the cigar should rest against the base of your fingers and is held in place by your thumb.

Separate your left fingers a bit, then interlace your right fingers between your left fingers. This is done in a special way because your right second finger remains outside of the interlacing. This is the breakdown: Your right first finger slides between your left first and second fingers. Your right second finger slides onto the shaft of the cigar as your right third finger slides between your left second and third finger. Your right fourth finger slides between your left third and fourth fingers.

This interlacing of fingers must be done quickly and smoothly. Once your fingers are interlaced, keep them clasped tightly in "prayer" position as your thumbs rest against the sides of the upright cigar. Let fellow smokers see the situation as you say, *"I pray this works!"*

Move your thumbs away from the cigar and flatten your interlaced fingers. From the view of fellow smokers, the cigar seems magnetized or suspended. (Fig. 1)

(Fig. 1)

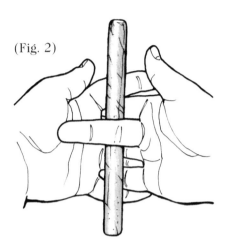

(Fig. 2)

If you were to count the visible fingers at this stage, only seven can be seen. The actual situation on the opposite side indicates the nature of the trick. (Fig. 2)

Shake your hands up and down as though you were trying to dislodge the cigar. Ask someone to say, *"Drop!"* When he does, curl your right second finger inward and let the cigar fall to the table. When someone picks up the cigar, separate your hands to destroy any evidence of your trickery.

If you like, begin with the cigar in your mouth. Get your hands into the prayer position with your right second finger free and hidden behind your interlaced fingers. Now raise your interlaced fingers to grasp the cigar, secretly sliding it *under* your right second finger, then proceed as explained. Or, you can do the suspension, then, while the cigar is still behind your clasped hands, move your hands up to your mouth and guide the top end of the cigar between your lips.

SEVEN GETS YOU ONE

This will prove that you are on a first-name basis with the Amazing Kreskin, world-famous psychic.

WHAT YOU SEE You place seven cigar tubes on the table. Six of them contain a cigar and one is empty. You and another person freely mix them, then take turns choosing pairs and eliminating one until only one tube remains. The final tube is given to the spectator, who finds it the only tube without a cigar!

WHAT YOU NEED (1) Seven duplicate aluminum cigar holders. (2) Six cigars that fit inside the holders.

HOW IT WORKS Place the cigars in six of the holders and cap them. Place a rolled up paper about the same weight as the cigars in the seventh tube. Put a small mark or dent on this tube so that you can identify it.

Your objective is to eliminate all the cigar tubes except the empty one. This is done by a clever procedure devised by magician Roy Baker. It gives the impression that the picker actually is part of a random process whereby holders are eliminated.

Begin by explaining the premise. Explain that your friend has a wonderful opportunity to win one of the six cigars if he remains unaffected by the "silent psychic influence" you plan to exert.

Place the tubes on the table and mix them. Ask the spectator to do the same, then place them in a row and determine which one has the mark.

Pick up any two other tubes with each hand and ask your unsuspecting friend to eliminate one. Ask him to pick up any two tubes. Say, *"You have now freely chosen two and I get a chance to eliminate one. As you can see, the procedure is pretty haphazard."* If he does not pick up the marked one when he chooses his pair, you can eliminate either tube. If he happens to choose the marked one, eliminate the other one. This keeps the bogus tube in play.

Repeat this process by alternately picking up pairs and eliminating one. As you can see, this process does not permit your friend to ever eliminate the bogus tube. In fact, you get to make the last decision with the last pair. Needless to say, you eliminate the tube with the cigar and give the bogus tube to your friend.

Say, *"Open the tube and see what you have won!"* If you want to be a generous person, reverse the outcome so that your friend wins the cigar. In this case, use six bogus tubes and place the only cigar in the marked tube.

IMMOBILE CIGAR

Here's the perfect trick for your pocket square.

WHAT YOU SEE	You drape a handkerchief over your left hand and then place a cigar in its center. It is held by your thumb and fingers underneath and through the fabric. Your right hand grabs the hem of the handkerchief and yanks it free. The cigar apparently penetrates the cloth, remaining immobile and upright between your thumb and fingers.
WHAT YOU NEED	(1) A regular man's handkerchief. This may be silk square as long as it is opaque. (2) A cigar.
HOW IT WORKS	Keep your cigar in your mouth and hold the adjacent (not diagonal) corners of the handkerchief between your hands. Show both sides, then hold it by one corner with your right hand.

Drape it over your left hand with your fingertips pointing upward toward the ceiling. (Fig. 1) As you adjust the handkerchief, contrive to get your left thumb and pinky outside and behind the cloth. (Fig. 2) Everything looks copacetic from the front.

(Fig. 1)

(Fig. 2)

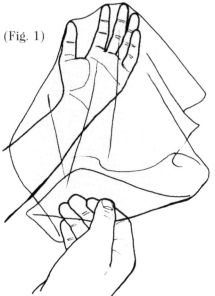

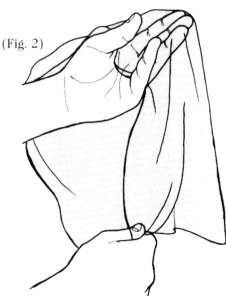

(Fig. 3)

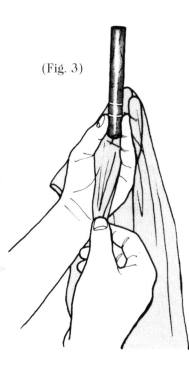

Remove the cigar from your mouth with your right hand and apparently place it upright in the center of the handkerchief. In reality, the unlit end is placed between your left thumb and pinky. The spectator thinks you are holding the cigar through the fabric. Again, everything looks normal.

Say, *"It doesn't matter what I do with the handkerchief, the cigar remains immobile!"* Grasp the hem that is between your left thumb and fourth finger at the back end.
Pull it down, then to the right. (Fig. 3) A silk square works smoothly and from the spectator's viewpoint, the action looks quite strange because the cigar remains immobile and the silk moves.

If you prefer, use a smaller cigarillo instead of a thicker cigar.

BLUFF STRETCH

A classic optical illusion.

WHAT YOU SEE You place two cigars on the table in a T-formation. You pick up one and seemingly stretch it. When it is placed next to the other cigar it is significantly longer.

WHAT YOU NEED Two similar-looking cigars, but one must be at least an inch longer.

HOW IT WORKS Remove the cigar-band from one and leave the other one in place.

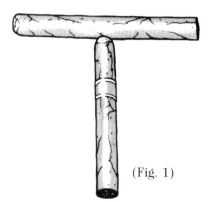

Place the longer cigar horizontally above the vertical, shorter one. (Fig. 1) Due to the nature of this optical illusion, both cigars will appear to be the same length. Say, *"Which cigar do you think tastes better?"* Since this is a rhetorical question, it does not matter what the victim replies. Be agreeable.

(Fig. 1)

Say, *"Which cigar do you think will take longer to smoke?"* This is a moot point, but regardless of the answer, pick up the top (longer) cigar and pretend to stretch it. Continue: *"Actually this one now has thirty more puffs to it. It is much longer!"*

Place it next to the shorter cigar so that both are vertical and side-by-side. (Fig. 2) As mentioned at the outset, this evokes a stronger response than you might expect. Try it when conversation lags. It is particularly strong in the wee hours of the morning and after several malt Scotches.

(Fig. 2)

44

CLOSE, BUT NO CIGAR

This is based on a concept by Peter Kane, the brilliant English magician.

WHAT YOU SEE You introduce an expensive cigar and the Ace through Five of Hearts. You explain that you are going to play a little game. After you explain the rules and the number of random choices the spectator is allowed, the game proceeds. The spectator places the cigar on one of the cards—say, the Five of Hearts. Since the card is a Five, the spectator makes five random moves. This is repeated two more times. Each time the spectator makes the number of moves equal to the value of the card landed on.

You turn over the other cards to show the same message: WINNER. When the spectator turns over the card under the cigar, it reads: CLOSE, BUT NO CIGAR! You pick up the cigar, smile, and smoke it.

WHAT YOU NEED (1) Five playing cards—Ace through Five of Hearts. (2) A very expensive cigar. (3) A marking pen.

HOW IT WORKS Take the marking pen and write in bold letters on the backs of the Ace, Three, and Five of Hearts: WINNER. On the backs of the Two and Four of Hearts write: CLOSE, BUT NO CIGAR. (Fig. 1)

(Fig. 1)

Deal the five cards face up in a row from Ace to Five of Hearts.

Explain to the spectator that he or she has three chances to win the high-quality cigar. Say, *"This is how the game works. You begin by placing the cigar on any one of the cards. Notice that the cards have a numerical value from one to five, the Ace being one. The subsequent number of moves you make is determined by the value of any given card. For example, if you place the cigar on the Three of Diamonds, you will subsequently make three moves. Understand?"*

45

Further explain that a move consists of moving from one card to the next, moving in any direction (right or left) each time. In this example, the cigar could be moved back and forth three times or simply moved two to the left and back to the right one move, ending up on the Two of Hearts. (Fig. 2)

(Fig. 2)

This procedure is done *three* times. Each time the number of moves is determined by the value of the card the cigar ends up on after a series of moves. Regardless of where the spectator begins and regardless of which direction he jumps, at the end of three procedures, the cigar will end up on the Two or Four of Hearts. These two cards are the CLOSE, BUT NO CIGAR cards.

Suppose the spectator ends up on the Four of Hearts. Pick up the Ace of Hearts with your right hand and place it face up in your left hand. Pick up the Three of Hearts with your right hand and place it face up on top of the Ace of Hearts. Pick up the Two of Hearts next and place it face up on the others, then finally place the Five of Hearts face up on top of all. The order of the cards from the top (face) should be: 5H-2H-3H-AH. The CLOSE, BUT NO CIGAR card is second from the top.

You are now going to apparently show the backs of these cards. Push over the 5H with your left thumb and grasp its inner right corner with your right thumb and forefinger. (Fig. 3)

(Fig. 3)

Turn both hands palm down to show the backside of their respective cards. The spectator will see two WINNER cards. (Fig. 4) Say, *"These two are winners!"* Turn your hands palm up again, then place the right-hand Five of Hearts onto the table as your left thumb pushes the Two of Hearts face up to the table.

(Fig. 4)

Take the Three of Hearts face up into your right hand and turn both hands palm down again to show two WINNER cards, saying: *"These two are also winners!"* Turn both hands palm up and drop the Three of Hearts and Ace of Hearts face up to the table. You have apparently shown the backs of all four cards, showing WINNER cards. In reality, you hid the back of one card. Look at the spectator and ask him to turn over the randomly selected card under the cigar. As everyone reads CLOSE, BUT NO CIGAR, quickly pick up the real cigar, light it, and add, *"The winner gets the smoke!"*

If you are a charitable person, you can rig this game to favor the spectator and make him a winner. Simply change around the words on the backs of the principal cards.

AMAZING CIGAR
FACTOID

Cigars were originally sold in bundles, covered with pigs' bladders. A pod or two of vanilla was added to improve the odor. Later, manufacturers used large cedar chests that could hold up to 10,000 cigars.

NICKEL CIGAR

"What this country needs is a good five-cent cigar."
—Thomas Marshall, Vice President of the United States (1914-1921)

This is a great visual gag. Nate Leipzig, a renowned vaudeville magician, performed a skillful version of this mystery by producing more than one cigar from a change purse. He also handed out the change purse at different times for examination.

WHAT YOU SEE   You compare the virtues and prices of several cigars and ask, "Who said, *'What this country needs is a good five-cent cigar'?"* You remove a small change purse and remove a nickel. You show the nickel and hand it to someone, adding: *"Well, that fellow was right!"* You then reach into the purse and remove a full-size cigar.

WHAT YOU NEED   (1) A cigar. (2) A nickel. (3) A small leather-type change purse with a clasp opening. (4) Nerve. In the old days, magicians called audacity "bold address."

HOW IT WORKS   Make a slit in the bottom of the purse large enough to accommodate the passage of a cigar. Put the nickel inside, then place the purse in your left (side) coat pocket and drop the cigar into your left sleeve.

Bring the conversation around to the Thomas Marshall quotation about five-cent cigars. As you talk, casually show that your hands are empty. Reach in your side coat pocket, remove the purse, and hold it with your left thumb and first finger. Reach in and remove the nickel. Hand it to a nearby victim.

While you and everybody looks at the nickel, drop your left hand to your side. Curl your fingers inward so that when the cigar in your sleeve drops due to gravity, its leading end is caught by your curled fingers. The purse is still retained by your thumb and first finger.

Raise your left hand about waist level so that only the top half of the purse can be seen. The cigar is held just below the purse in your palm. Your left thumb keeps the purse and cigar in place. The other end of the cigar is hidden by the lower part of your palm and wrist.

Open the clasp with your right hand, then reach inside and through the slit. Grab the leading end of the cigar and pull it out of the purse. (Fig. 1) Say, *"This one looks like a superb value."* Plunk the cigar between your lips and place the purse back into your pocket.

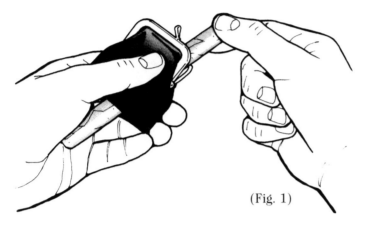

(Fig. 1)

OLD GELLER

Uri Geller, spoon-bender and psychic charmer, claims to restart broken watches, bend metal with his mind, and make things go bump in broad daylight. The ability to move objects with only your mind is called psychokinesis. Try psychokinesis with a cigar.

WHAT YOU SEE You place a cigar on the table or bar top and explain the Geller effect. You place your hand in front of the cigar and say, *"Through the power of mind over matter...I don't mind...and it doesn't matter...I will cause the cigar to roll toward me!"* Without further ado, the cigar rolls away from your hand and toward you.

WHAT YOU NEED (1) A small, nicely rounded cigar. (2) A good set of lungs.

HOW IT WORKS Place the cigar on a smooth surface between you and your flat hand. Keep your fingers together because your hand will be a "wall" that permits this deceit to happen.

Tell the fellow smokers to concentrate on the cigar. You must now blow a stream of air against your hand. (Fig. 1) This must be a subtle, steady stream, perfectly directed. Lean toward the cigar and your hand as though you were concentrating your psychic energy. When you accurately blow against your hand, the air bounces off and hits the cigar. The cigar will roll in the *opposite* direction *toward* you.

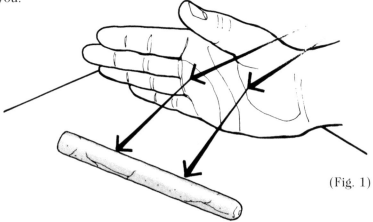

(Fig. 1)

A more elaborate version is to use two cigars. Place them about an inch apart on a smooth surface. Point your right forefinger and trace an imaginary circle around the cigars. Keep tracing this circle, ostensibly to centralize your psychic energy. In the process, direct your secret stream of air *between* the cigars. The cigars will roll apart, moving in opposite directions. Be serious. Do *not* be a blowhard or you will, as Giovanni says, "blow the trick!"

AMAZING CIGAR
FACTOID

Groucho Marx said, "If you forget a line, all you have to do is stick the cigar in your mouth and puff on it until you can think of what you've forgotten." Carnival pitchman call this a "stall," which also explains why many of them smoked cigars.

PUNCTURE JUNCTURE

This is a strong solid-through-solid stunt.

WHAT YOU SEE You place a cocktail napkin over your left fist and then make a "well" or indentation in the center with your right thumb. An upright cigar is placed into the "well" and its top end is suddenly slammed downward. It seemingly tears through the napkin and drops onto the table. The whole thing turns out to be an illusion because the napkin is shown to be whole and undamaged.

WHAT YOU NEED (1) A cigar. (2) A cocktail napkin.

HOW IT WORKS You actually place the napkin over your left fist so that its center is directly over the "well" formed by your curled fingers and thumb at the top of your fist. Your right thumb comes over to apparently push in the top part of the napkin to form this indentation or "well." However, your thumb, pointing downward toward the floor, initially moves against your left fist from the backside. Your left fingers open the fist slightly so that a secret "tunnel" is formed at the back. (Fig. 1)

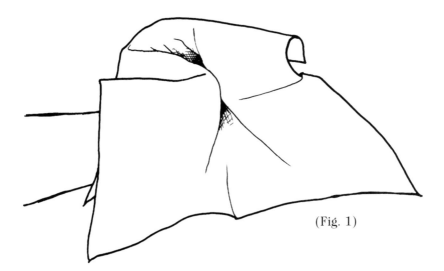

(Fig. 1)

The drawing shows how the actual condition looks with the hand and cigar removed. From the front, everything looks normal. You can close your left fingers again and bring the napkin into a shape that looks fair and aboveboard.

Position the upright cigar part way into the formed "tunnel," then strike your flat right hand against the top end of the cigar. (Fig. 2) The cigar will freely drop through the "tunnel" and the napkin will be undamaged.

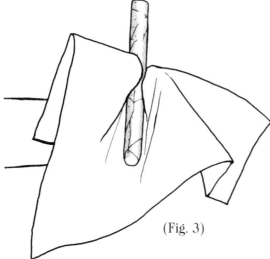

(Fig. 2)

(Fig. 3)

Figure 3 is an exposed view of how the cigar moves through the napkin. The left fingers except for the thumb and forefinger are held open to expose the "work."

After the cigar hits the table, lightly crumple the napkin into a ball and say, *"Be healed!"* Then gradually open and show it whole. Everything may be examined.

MISTER BLISTER

This feat can be done as a quick oddity, but if played right, it resonates in the minds of others for years.

WHAT YOU SEE

Someone starts talking about the latest New Age fad, book, or therapy and you gaze at your cigar and say, *"Ever since I started smoking cigars, I've transcended pain. This fantastic smoke releases so many endorphins, that I feel nothing but pleasure."* You then hold the ends of your lit cigar between your thumb and forefinger, with the scorching end against your thumb. You proudly display your prized smoke as though it were a healing wand, holding it for about twenty seconds...to the gradually increasing horror of your fellow smokers. Finally, you place the cigar back in your mouth, smile, and add: *"The temperature of the lit end of a cigar is over 250 degrees, yet it does not hurt..."* You then extend your thumb to reveal a large, red blister.

"Sometimes a blister forms," you matter-of-factly continue, *"but this is healed by the ashes of my cigar."* You place some ashes onto the blister and ask someone to place a fingertip against your thumb. After some rubbing and deep, blissful concentration, the spectator's finger is removed and your thumb is healed. The blister is gone!

WHAT YOU NEED

(1) Any key with a round or oval opening at its top. (Fig. 1) You can also use a round washer, easily found in any hardware store. (2) A drinking glass filled with an iced beverage. (3) A lit cigar.

(Fig. 1)

HOW IT WORKS

At an opportune moment, place the head of the key on the fleshy pad of your right thumb. (Fig. 2) Press the key and your thumb against any hard surface or use your opposing right forefinger. Firmly squeeze for about 15-20 seconds—long enough to indent the skin of your thumb and form an oval bas-relief that looks exactly like a reddish, fresh blister when the key is removed. (Fig. 3) This blister-like form will remain for a minute or two.

(Fig. 2)

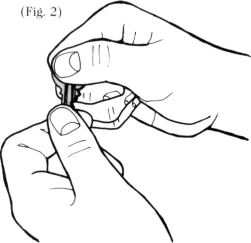

You must also lower the temperature of your "blistered" thumb. This prevents you from burning your skin. This is done by pressing it against the side of your chilled drinking glass. Or, while no one is looking, press your prepared thumb against a chunk of ice for several seconds.

(Fig. 3)

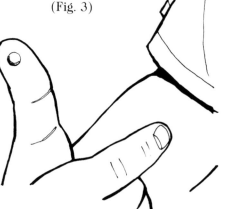

When you have conversationally set the stage and your right thumb is fully prepared, remove your lit cigar. (Caution! Allow your cigar to cool a bit. Do not puff on it; leave it resting on an ashtray for a few minutes.) Finally, hold the cigar by its ends so that the lit end is against your "blistered" thumb. (Fig. 4) Display it with a bit of bravado.

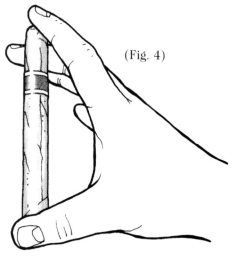

(Fig. 4)

You will be able to hold the cigar in this bizarre fashion for at least ten seconds without actually burning your thumb. The heat differential permits this to happen without burning your skin. When you feel the temperature rising in your thumb, casually remove the cigar with your left hand and replace it in your mouth. Let the sensation of heat in your thumb be your guide. Be careful. When you feel the heat, remove the cigar.

After about ten seconds have elapsed and you have acted calm and collected, you can either remain calm throughout (as suggested in "What You See") or you can suddenly pretend that you have finally burnt your thumb. Jerk the cigar away with your left hand and let out a yelp. Look at your thumb and curse. The faces of your fellow smokers will register alarm or delight, depending on their personalities. Many will think that you are crazy, but everyone has been primed to *fully* suspend their disbelief.

You will have everyone's rapt attention. Place some ashes from your ashtray onto your thumb, then have the spectator rub the ashes on your thumb. Stare at your thumb and say, *"Heal!"* Continue in this manner until the ashes fall away and the "blister" gradually disappears. When it does, you have made a crazy feat dramatically memorable. Smile and continue smoking your cigar.

For those of you who are a bit timid about actually touching the hot end of a cigar, simply fake the action. You can still get a good reaction.

GONE!

This is an apt after-dinner quickie where you can make your cigar disappear without smoking it.

WHAT YOU SEE	You are holding a cigar between your hands. Slowly you press your hands together and the cigar crumples into nothingness.
WHAT YOU NEED	(1) A cigar. (2) A table.
HOW IT WORKS	You must be seated at a table. Hold the ends of the cigar against your palms so that the cigar is held in a horizontal position. Momentarily rest the underside of your hands on the table near the rear edge. (Fig. 1)

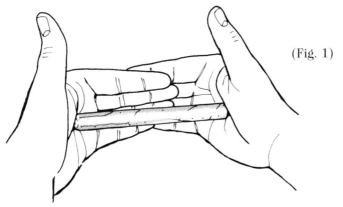

(Fig. 1)

Raise your hands upward about chest level and enfold the fingers of both hands in front of the cigar to hide it from view. (Fig. 2) Open your fingers again and resume the starting position, again showing the cigar. Lower your hands to the table.

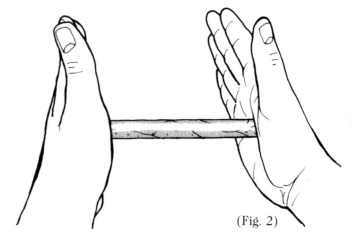

(Fig. 2)

Cover the front of the cigar again with your fingers and raise them to chest level. Open your fingers to the starting position and show the cigar again. Cover with your fingers and lower both hands to the table.

When the underside of your hands rests against the table, release the cigar and let it drop in your lap. Pretend that you are still holding the cigar, then raise your hands again with your fingers hiding the fact that the cigar is no longer in place.

Move your hands forward slightly, then pretend to slowly crumple the non-existent cigar between your hands. Eventually show that it has vanished.

CIGAR FU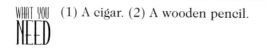

This macho stunt is for special occasions. If conversation happens to drift towa~~rd~~ the martial arts, Jackie Chan, or any of the chop-and-block films popularized ~~by~~ Bruce Lee, you can show your strange prowess with a cigar.

WHAT YOU SEE	You have someone hold both ends of a pencil so that it is parallel to the floor. You then hold your cigar in one hand so that it is extended like a sword. You say, *"Not only is this cigar a great smoke, but it's a lethal weapon!"* You perform a bow and yell *"Hi-Ya!"* as you suddenly hit the pencil with the shaft of your cigar and the pencil breaks in half. The cigar is unharmed.

WHAT YOU NEED	(1) A cigar. (2) A wooden pencil.

58

HOW
IT WORKS

This is done by cheating. Hold your cigar in readiness for the downward sweep. (Fig. 1) Explain what you are going to attempt and ask the spectator to hold the ends of the pencil tightly.

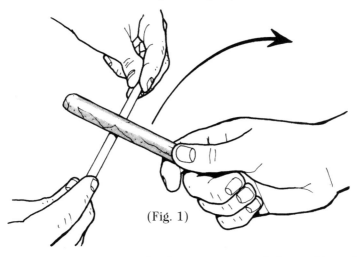

(Fig. 1)

Pretend to concentrate. During the larger motion of the sudden, downward sweep of your hand, you sneakily extend your forefinger. It moves under the cigar and strikes the center of the pencil during the swift, downward sweep. (Fig. 2) Yell out, *"Hi-Ya!"*

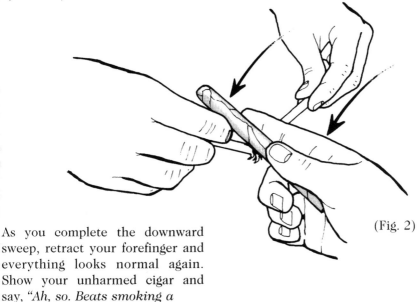

(Fig. 2)

As you complete the downward sweep, retract your forefinger and everything looks normal again. Show your unharmed cigar and say, *"Ah, so. Beats smoking a pencil any day!"*

PENTAGAR

If you are a collector of fine writing implements and a smoker of fine cigars, this trick is right up your alley.

WHAT YOU SEE You show a handkerchief and pen, then wrap the pen in the handkerchief. When it is unwrapped, the pen has changed into a cigar.

WHAT YOU NEED (1) A cigar. (2) An opaque handkerchief or dinner table napkin. (3) A pen about the size of a small cigar.

HOW IT WORKS Prior to performance spread out the napkin on the table with the cigar hidden underneath.

The pen on the dinner napkin is next to the cigar underneath. Rotate the pen and cigar so that their ends point east and west. Fold the south corner of the napkin up to the north corner but not flush. The original north corner extends past the south corner about an inch. (Fig. 1—shown from the spectator's point of view) Do this without being too conspicuous or studied. Place your palms flat on the pen and cigar (through the cloth). Roll the creased part of the handkerchief inward in a counter-clockwise direction so that it enfolds *under* the cigar.

Keep rolling the napkin in this fashion, more or less rolling it into a tube, until only the original north and south corners remain at the top. Then let the north corner rotate around once, essentially *changing places* with the south corner.

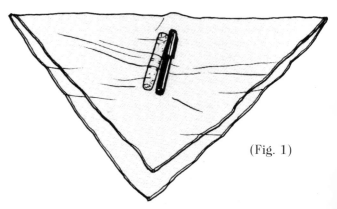

(Fig. 1)

If you pull these exposed corners in *opposite directions*, the napkin will unfurl. However, it is now turned over and the cigar is uppermost and the pen is underneath. Hand the cigar to someone, then grab the middle of the handkerchief and the pen concealed underneath with your left hand. Place it in your lap or pocket to get rid of the evidence.

RISING TO THE OCCASION

People will think your cigar is possessed.

 WHAT YOU SEE You remove a cigar tube and remove the top. Holding the tube with one hand, you extend it toward a fellow smoker and the cigar inside slowly rises upwards.

 WHAT YOU NEED (1) A cigar that is packaged in a glass or aluminum tube. (2) A length of nylon or cloth thread. (3) A small button. (4) A bent pin.

HOW IT WORKS Affix an end of the thread to the head of the bent pin and sew the button onto the other end. The length of the thread is determined by experimentation, although it must be as long as the length of the tube, plus about an inch.

Insert the pin into an end of the cigar so it stays firmly in place. Place this end into the tube and let the button-end hang over the top lip of the tube. Place the lid on.

Remove the tube and hold it in your right hand so that the hanging button is at the back and cannot be seen.

Remove the lid with your left hand, then place your right thumb at the back of the tube against the hanging button. Except for a short piece of thread, there is very little to see from any angle.

To cause the cigar to rise, simply pull the button down with your right thumb. (Fig. 1)

(Fig. 1)

59

THE BAND PLAYS ON

BAND DANCE

This presentation was popularized by Martin Gardner, who for many years wrote a mathematical recreations column in the *Scientific American*. Its unique feature is that you carefully explain and actually demonstrate in slow motion exactly how the trick is *apparently* done. Yet after you finish, your spectators will vainly try to duplicate your actions. They will not be able to do it, no matter how many hours they practice.

WHAT YOU SEE

A cigar band instantly hops or "dances" from the tip of your second finger to the tip of your first finger and back again. You explain that by slightly lifting your forefinger, you press your thumb on the left side of the band, then by pressing your third finger against the other side, you can securely hold the band. By merely extracting the tip of your second finger and inserting the tip of your first finger into the band, the transposition is completed. By holding the band in the same way, the process is reversed and the band is brought back to its original position. These moves are demonstrated in slow motion until everyone understands them.

To show the effect in action, you place your right first and second fingers together against your outstretched left arm at the bend of your elbow. The cigar band is on the tip of your second finger. Your thumb, third and fourth fingers are curled into your palm. While you quickly tap your two outstretched fingers at a point on your forearm just beyond the bend of your elbow, the cigar band seems to jump to the tip of your first finger. With a second quick tap, the cigar band instantaneously jumps back to the tip of your second finger.

The effect is pretty and spectators will want to try it. However, they will discover that when they hold the band as explained, the required manipulation seems impossible. Yet you can repeat the transposition of the band from fingertip to fingertip at lightning speed. Onlookers will be impressed with the delicacy and agility of your fingers.

WHAT YOU NEED

(1) A cigar band. (2) Fast fingers.

HOW IT WORKS

Place a cigar band onto your right second finger just beneath your fingernail.

The so-called explanation is pure misdirection. The real secret is more subtle. The band does *not* move from its position on the tip of your second finger. It is an optical illusion. At the start of the action, show your first and second fingers, outstretched and together, pressed against your left arm at the bend of the elbow. Your third and fourth fingers are bent into your palm and the cigar band is at the tip of your second finger. (Fig. 1)

In the action of tapping your fingers, simply bend your *first* finger into the palm and extend your third finger. (Fig. 2) The larger motion of the tapping covers the smaller movements of your fingers. The spectators will be staring at the *position* of the band and will not notice the change of your fingers.

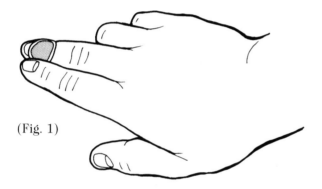

(Fig. 1)

Let the spectator note the apparent transposition, but do not linger. Repeat the tapping movement of your right hand while simultaneously stretching out your first finger and bending your third finger into the palm again. The band seems to jump back to the tip of your second finger. If you like, you can separate your fingers to a V-shape.

Martin Gardner writes, "The curious thing is that the so-called explanation of the trick is accepted and it is amusing to watch the vain attempts made to duplicate the trick by using the suggested moves."

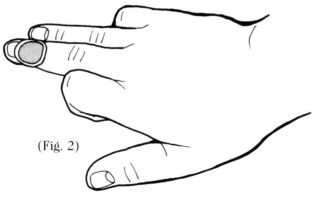

(Fig. 2)

ON THE UP AND UP

This may be the coolest trick in the book.

WHAT YOU SEE
You show a cigar band and a length of broken rubber band. The cigar band is threaded onto the rubber band, which is held between your hands so that the rubber band is angled upward. The cigar band is at the lower end. Then by apparently using the power of psychokinesis (the ability to move objects with your mind), you cause the cigar band to *move up* the rubber band and against the countervailing force of gravity.

WHAT YOU NEED
(1) A rubber band, which is broken into a single strand. (2) A cigar band.

HOW IT WORKS
Thread the cigar band onto the center of the rubber band, then grasp the rubber band about four inches above the end to be held by your left thumb and forefinger. Your right thumb and forefinger hold the other end.

Stretch the strand between both hands so that it is taut. Hold it at an angle so that the band is near the lower part. (Fig. 1) (The diagrams show an exposed view in the left hand.) The angle is about 45 degrees and the excess part of the lower end is held inside your curled left fingers. The excess band is concealed in your left hand.

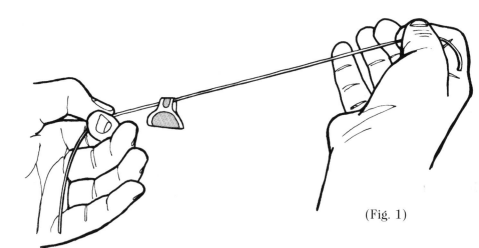

(Fig. 1)

Your friends will see the hanging cigar band. They will then eventually see the cigar band seemingly *slide upward* toward your right hand. The movement is slow and spooky. (Fig. 2)

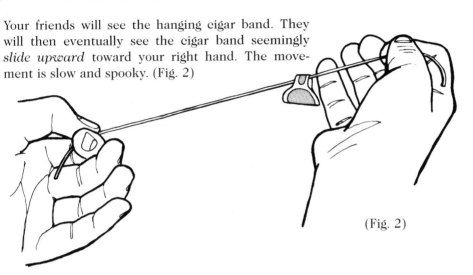

(Fig. 2)

In reality, the cigar band remains *stationary*. What really happens is that your left thumb and forefinger gradually relax their grip on the taut rubber band. The excess part of the rubber band imperceptibly slides past your left thumb and forefinger as the degree of tautness lessens. The rubber band loosens and the cigar band, held in place by friction, moves along *with* the relaxing band. The illusion that the cigar band is moving is convincing.

The relaxation of the rubber band's tension cannot be detected. The cigar band seems to slide *upward* against the force of gravity. When the cigar band gets to the top of the "incline," toss everything to the table for examination. A key element is to keep both hands absolutely still and stationary. Let the rubber band do all the work.

BAND SCAPE

This was originated by a Chicago magician named Russ Walsh. In the dark ages, they burned witches at the stake for less.

WHAT YOU SEE You remove your favorite cigar from your pocket, remove its cellophane wrapper, and twist it into a short string-like shape. You take off the cigar band from the cigar and ask the spectator to place it onto the cellophane as though he were threading a ring onto a string. Have the spectator hold the cellophane-string by both ends, whereupon you cover the band and cellophane with a handkerchief or napkin. The band is then magically removed from the cellophane without tearing or cutting the band or wrapper. Everything can be examined.

THE AMAZING CIGAR

WHAT YOU NEED (1) A cigar wrapped in cellophane. (2) A duplicate cigar band that matches the one on your cigar. (3) A handkerchief or napkin.

HOW IT WORKS Place the duplicate cigar band in your right trouser or coat pocket with a pocket-handkerchief. If you are performing at a bar or dinner table, use a table napkin or a couple of bar napkins.

Remove the cellophane wrapper from a cigar and twist it tightly to form a solid, string-like tube. Have the spectator hold it as you gingerly remove the cigar band carefully. Do not tear it. Give it to the spectator, ask him to thread it onto the cellophane-string, then have him hold the ends with each hand. (Fig. 1) Say, *"Hold tightly and do not let go of either end! I'm going to show you something impossible!"*

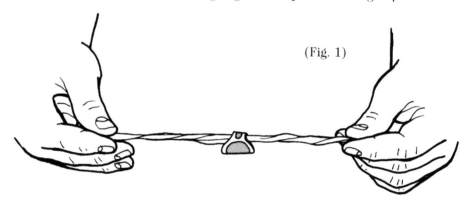

(Fig. 1)

Reach into your pocket, supposedly to get your handkerchief. In the process, obtain the duplicate cigar band and hold it in your curled second, third, and fourth fingers. Do not try anything fancy. Take advantage of the fact that you normally curl your fingers to hold a handkerchief. This provides ample cover. If you use a bar or table napkin, when you pick it up to unwrap it and smooth it out, there is a reason to keep your fingers curled.

Place the handkerchief or napkin over the cigar band and cellophane-string. Reach underneath with both hands and surreptitiously tear the original cigar band and remove it. Quietly crumple it into a small ball, then position the duplicate cigar band at your left thumb and fingertips and curl your right fingers around the torn cigar band. Remove the handkerchief or napkin with your right hand and display the whole cigar band in your left hand.

Hand the *whole* cigar band to the spectator as your right hand places the handkerchief and hidden torn cigar band in your right pocket. Everything may be examined.

OFF AGAIN, ON AGAIN

This requires some practice, but the swindle has been used by tricksters for over a century. Do not pass this up.

WHAT YOU SEE
You show a cigar and explain that it affects your eyes. The cigar band disappears and reappears a few times, then magically jumps from one end to the other.

WHAT YOU NEED
(1) A cigar with its band still intact and encircling it. (2) A matching band. (3) A small piece of aluminum. (4) Glue.

HOW IT WORKS
The fake used in this feat is a *half-band* that can be clipped onto the cigar. This is made by carefully cutting a band in half so that its logo remains. This is then glued onto a thin piece of aluminum. When you remove the aluminum top off any tube of potato chips, keep this metal. Trim it to the exact size of the band, then super-glue the paper band on top. After it dries, you can shape the band to form a miniature clip that will stay on a cigar without falling off, yet can be easily slipped off when necessary.

Remove the cellophane wrapper from the cigar, then gingerly slide the real band about an inch from an end. Clip the fake band on the cigar near the other end.

Hold the end with the real band between your right thumb, first, and second fingers. Your thumb conceals the real band. Rotate the cigar so that the half-fake shows uppermost. (Fig. 1)

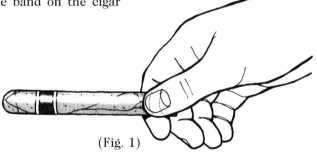

(Fig. 1)

Show the cigar and ask, *"Have you ever smoked one of these? It's called an Optica...not Optimo, but Optica. It makes you see things that aren't there!"* The next action is an old swindle. When you flick your right hand up and down, you imperceptibly roll the cigar a half turn between your thumb and forefinger. The larger action covers the smaller action. On the downstroke of the "flick," the band will seem to disappear. (Fig. 2)

Your victim sees only an unadorned cigar; the half-band is now under the cigar. To make the band reappear, simply reverse the process. Do this a couple of times, then add: *"See what I mean?"*

(Fig. 2)

Finally, while still holding the cigar in your right hand when the fake is on top and showing, rotate it end-over-end with your left hand. Grasp the turning end with the fake in your right hand. When it turns, the fake will be underneath and the real band on the other end comes into view. This is startling.

Take the cigar out of your right hand with your left, leaving the fake in your curled right fingers. Hand it to your victim to inspect or smoke. As your right hand reaches into your coat pocket for a lighter, leave the fake behind.

AMAZING CIGAR FACTOIDS

Myron Freedman's collection of cigar bands numbers about 60,000, covering the years 1890 to the present. With another cigar band collector, Harry Copleston, he wrote *The Cigar Band Catalogue*, which covers the history of the manufacturers. Freedman says about 125,000 different cigar bands were identified and discussed in his volume.

Catherine the Great had her cigars banded with silk. She did not want to touch the rough texture of the wrapper, so her courtesans bound the cigars with ribbons.

At one time a person could have his own private cigar brand, with a picture of his home, his family, his yacht, or a favorite pet.

HEAD TURNERS

SPARKY

This is fast, flashy, and weird.

WHAT YOU SEE	You hold your cigar like a giant match and strike the tuck against the striking surface of a matchbook. It suddenly ignites, apparently lighting itself.
WHAT YOU NEED	A wooden match cut in half, which is pushed into the tuck of the cigar so that only the head is partially visible.
HOW IT WORKS	Simply introduce the prepared cigar and keep it moving as you talk. Ask, *"Does anybody have a light?"* Before anyone can react, say: *"Never mind! I forgot that these cigars are self-lighting!"* The evidence will burn as you smoke.

Strike the tuck end of the cigar, namely the exposed match-head, against the striking surface of a matchbox. As soon as it ignites, puff on the head to fully ignite it.

FLAME THROWER

This will get the attention of everyone, including Smokey the Bear.

WHAT YOU SEE	Large flames shoot out from the tuck while your cigar is being lit.
WHAT YOU NEED	(1) A wooden match. (2) A cigar.
HOW IT WORKS	As you light the tuck of your cigar with a *wooden* match, rotating it in the flame, take in your first puff of smoke. As you continue holding the flame to the tuck, blow *back* through the cigar and into the flame. This will cause large flames to flare up.

AMAZING CIGAR QUOTE

"A cigar is a fire on one end and a fool on the other."

—*Horace Greeley*

ROTATION

This is a head-turning quickie designed to elicit a double take. The onlooker sees it, then is not quite sure what he saw and says, *"Wanna run that by me again?"* This sight gag was used by many vaudeville comedians.

WHAT YOU SEE

You are happily smoking your cigar. When you notice that someone is looking at you, you seemingly remove and rotate your cigar 180 degrees and replace it in your mouth. If you actually did this, the lit end would end up in your mouth. In reality, the cigar ends up in the correct smoking position.

WHAT YOU NEED

A lit cigar.

HOW IT WORKS

Grasp your cigar underhanded between your right first and second fingers with your thumb on top. (Fig. 1)

(Fig. 1)

Remove the cigar from your lips and apparently rotate it end-over-end or 180 degrees in a counter-clockwise direction. In reality, the cigar is given a quick, complete (360 degrees) revolution.

Simply clip the cigar between your right first and second fingers (like a baton twirler) and when it has rotated 180 degrees and is parallel to the floor, use your right thumb to effect the rest of the rotation as your right palm ends up toward the fellow smokers. (Fig. 2)

Place the cigar back in your mouth. Instead of having the lit end between your lips, it is at the intended far end. Puffs between spins adds to the overall effect.

(Fig. 2)

BUTT HEAD

Here's a tasty treat that will make your friends do a double take.

WHAT YOU SEE	After you have finished smoking your fine cigar, you announce to your friends that you cannot bear to waste one inch. You then promptly remove the band from your cigar and chew and swallow the cigar butt.
WHAT YOU NEED	(1) A cigar butt. (2) An overcooked mini eggroll. (3) Duplicate cigar band.
HOW IT WORKS	This requires a little preparation, but if you like self-incriminating practical jokes, this is worth the extra time and trouble. Visit your neighborhood food market and buy hors oeuvres-sized frozen egg rolls. Over-bake them until they are darker then normal or the brownish color of your cigar. Next, take your lighter and char the end to make it look like the ash. Place the duplicate cigar band around the egg roll in the appropriate position. You may need to adjust the cigar band with tape so it fits properly. Wrap the cigar butt decoy (egg roll) in a napkin and then place it in your jacket pocket. You are now ready to go!

After you have finished smoking your cigar, casually leave it in the ashtray and remove the decoy from your pocket when no one is paying attention to you. Treat the egg roll as if it were your real cigar. Hold it and say, *"This has been the best tasting cigar I have ever had."* Remove the band. *"So good, in fact, I don't want to waste an inch if it."* You then pop it in your mouth and munch away.

OLD BLACK
MATCH-IK

COMEBACK MATCH

This is one of the strongest mysteries you can perform with an ordinary book of matches. Do not underestimate its potency and guard its secret well.

WHAT YOU SEE
You open an ordinary book of matches and ask someone to count the matches. Suppose your victim counts seventeen matches. You openly tear out one of the matches and ask the victim to hold this seventeenth match for a moment. You close the book, take back the match, strike it against the book and light it, then you blow it out. The closed matchbook is given to your victim to hold. The *burnt* match suddenly disappears. The matchbook is opened and the burnt match has reappeared. The matches are counted. There are *exactly* seventeen matches. The *coup de grace* occurs when you ask the victim to *tear out* the burnt match. When he does, he sees that it had unmistakably reattached itself to the matchbook!

WHAT YOU NEED
An ordinary matchbook.

HOW IT WORKS
Before you begin, secretly bend back a match from the center of the front row. (Fig. 1) If it is a new matchbook with twenty matches in it, pull out about five or six matches from various places. Take one of these matches and light it, then use it to light the bent match. Immediately blow it out. Close the flap of the matchbook but leave the burnt one bent down.

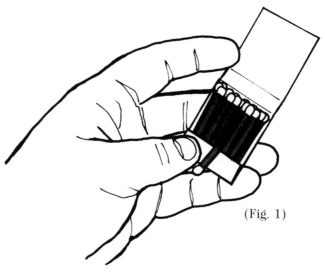

(Fig. 1)

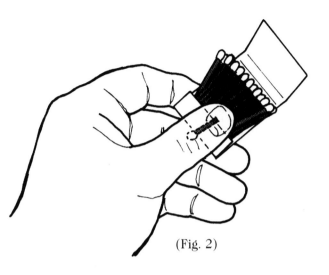

(Fig. 2)

Introduce the matchbook and open the flap. Cover the bent match with your left thumb. (Fig. 2) Count the matches to yourself and spread them out a bit. Suppose you count fourteen matches. Say, *"I count fourteen. I'm not too good at math, so will someone count the matches for me?"*

Extend the matchbook toward someone, but hold it tightly. When your victim has counted and corroborated that there are fourteen matches, openly pull out any match and hand it to your victim, saying: *"Here! Hold the fourteenth match, please!"* Look at the spectator and as you close the matchbook, tilting it back so that the matches are out of view, furtively push the bent, burnt match back in alignment with the others. Tuck in the flap, turn the matchbook over to expose the striking surface, then ask for the loose match.

Strike the loose match and ignite it. Immediately blow it out. Say, *"Please hold the matchbook tightly and hold it a little higher."* As you utter this harmless line, raise the spectator's hand that is holding the matchbook a few inches higher. This attracts attention. When everybody looks at the match book, lower your right hand and drop the burnt match to the floor (if you are standing) or in your lap (if you are sitting). Do not make a big deal of this drop off. Pretend that you are still holding the match in your right hand, by holding it in a fist.

Say, *"Watch the burnt match go!"* Make a throwing action toward the matchbook with your right hand. Stare at the matchbook and ask, *"Did you feel it?"* Ask the spectator to open the matchbook. The first surprise is about to happen. Watch everybody's face when they see the burnt match back in the matchbook.

Say, *"Count the matches, please!"* Watch their faces when your victim counts fourteen matches. This is the second surprise, but the killer is yet to come. Say, *"Please rip out the burnt match!"*

HEADLESS

This trick fooled Einstein. Not *the* Einstein, but a know-it-all friend, Morty Einstein, who fell for it and has not spoken to me since.

WHAT YOU SEE
You hold a wooden match with its *red* head pointing up in your left hand. Your right thumb and fingers pinch this head and apparently pull it off the match. Your victims cry foul and skeptically say that you merely turned the match end-for-end. With a look of great innocence, you show the other end. There is a head on it, but it is a *different color!*

WHAT YOU NEED
Two matches. One has a red head and the other has a different-colored head (blue or green). You can use wooden or paper matches.

HOW IT WORKS
Hold the redheaded match upright in your left hand. Your right hand secretly holds the other match upside down between your right thumb and second fingertip. (Fig. 1)

Say, *"Sometimes the heads on these matches are loose."* Reach over with your right hand and actually pinch the red head between your right thumb and forefinger. (Fig. 2) Suddenly move your right hand upward and do nothing. Keep your right thumb and fingers together in the same position.

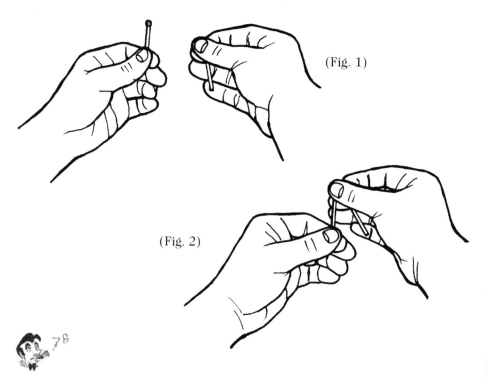

(Fig. 1)

(Fig. 2)

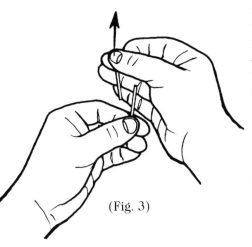

(Fig. 3)

Pretend that you failed to behead the match. Pinch the redheaded match again, only this time when you suddenly raise your right hand, *switch* matches. That is, leave the upside down match and lift away the redheaded one.
(Fig. 3)

Stare at the supposedly beheaded match as your right hand drops to a relaxed position on the table or in your lap. If it drops near the back edge of the table, simply drop it into your lap. Do not look at it and pay attention to anything except the beheaded match. Forget about it.

Wait for the skeptics to say something about turning the match end-over-end. If nobody says anything, say: *"Some killjoys think that I simply cheat and turn the match end-over-end."* Smile, then show the opposite end of the match and triumphantly add: *"Ah, yes, but now its head has a different color!"* Hand it to the most obvious skeptic.

AMAZING CIGAR FACTOIDS

Millions of matchbooks with bombs printed on them were dropped all over war-torn Europe by soldiers during World War II. The friction-strip used to light these matches was the backside of Hitler.

One of the interesting practices of Cuban cigar factories began in 1865 when books were read aloud to the rollers as they worked, including novels by Zola, Dumas, and Hugo. Consequently, cigar rollers were often the most literate people in their neighborhoods.

Mark Twain smoked five cigars a day on the porch of his home.

THIEVES AND SHEEP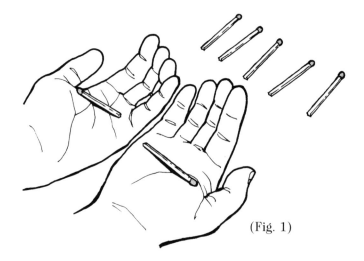

This is an old but interesting swindle. Although it is semi-automatic, it gives the impression that you are a master of sleight of hand or one sneaky fellow.

 WHAT YOU SEE

Seven wooden matches are placed on the table. Two are picked up, one in each hand. The five matches on the table represent sheep and the two in your hands represent thieves. The thieves see the sheep and conspire to steal them, even though the farmer's house is nearby. Nevertheless, they proceed to take the sheep one by one. You pick up the five matches that are on the table one at a time, alternating hands in the process. After the "sheep" are snugly in hand, you say: *"The thieves then see the lights in the farmer's house suddenly go on. This spooks them and they quickly replace the sheep,"* again alternating hands.

It was a false alarm and the lights in the house go out. The thieves again steal the "sheep" one by one, and again you pick up the matches by alternating hands. But suddenly the farmer appears and when he checks inside the two "barns" (hands), he finds that the two thieves are asleep in one and the five sheep are asleep in the other.

 WHAT YOU NEED

Seven wooden matches.

HOW IT WORKS

As stated at the outset, this trick is semi-automatic. Show the beginning setup. (Fig. 1)

(Fig. 1)

Begin by picking up the five matches that are on the table with your right hand. (Fig. 2) After you have picked up all five in this alternating manner, your *right* hand will be holding four matches and your left hand will be holding three.

(Fig. 2)

When you replace them, begin laying them down with your *left* hand. (Fig. 3) After five matches have been replaced, your left hand will be empty. However, pretend that you are still holding the original match. Keep your fist closed as though you are still holding it.

(Fig. 3)

Pick them up a second time, beginning with your right hand, which starts with two matches already in its clutches. Your victims will not notice the minor discrepancy of the alternating hands swindle. Open both hands simultaneously to show two in your left and five in your right. (Fig. 4) At the end, they will wonder how you sneakily transported one or more matches from hand to hand.

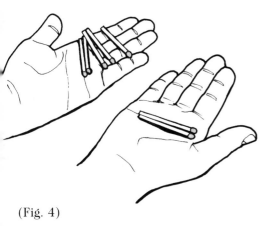

(Fig. 4)

POLTERGEIST BOOK

This is by New York magician and psychologist Ken Krenzel with some help from two other magicians named Jeff Busby and Ronald Dayton.

WHAT YOU SEE

An ordinary paper matchbook is placed flat on your open palm. You utter a quaint incantation and it begins to rotate in a *lateral* direction in a spooky manner. It is immediately handed out for examination.

WHAT YOU NEED

An ordinary matchbook.

HOW IT WORKS

The setup takes only a few seconds. Open the cover and fold one of the middle matches down over the edge of the short flap where the cover is usually tucked. Fold the cover over the matches. Do not engage its edge under the flap, but press it against the flap and then fold the bent match straight up or perpendicular to the matchbook.

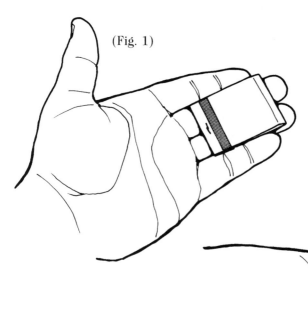

(Fig. 1)

Hold the matchbook on your outstretched fingers of your left hand with the top nearest the fingertips. (Fig. 1) The bent match, still perpendicular and pointing to the floor, is between the middle knuckles of your left second and third fingers. (Fig. 2)

(Fig. 2)

To make the matchbook turn, press your second and third fingers together. This forces the flat match, jammed by its *edges*, to twist between your knuckles. This, in turn, causes the matchbook to revolve 90 degrees in a clockwise direction. (Fig. 3)

A little experimentation will show where to grasp the match and how to squeeze it to get good results. Act surprised when the matchbook suddenly turns, then readjust the book to its original position with your other hand. This resets the matchbook for another movement. Make it spin again.

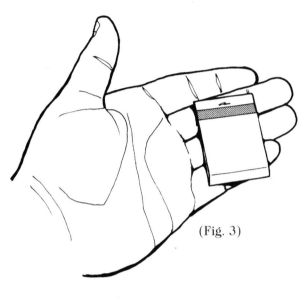

(Fig. 3)

Finally, grasp the top of the matchbook with your right hand and spread your left fingers to release the bent match. Raise the book to a vertical position with its other side toward the fellow smokers. Flip open the cover and secretly push the bent match straight to match its companions. Hand the matchbook for examination.

SNAP-BACK

This trick is in every boy's book of tricks. Nevertheless, the principle upon which it is based is enduring.

WHAT YOU SEE	You show a wooden match and place it under a handkerchief. The spectator feels the match under the handkerchief and is asked to break it. Afterwards, the hand is opened to reveal a whole match, restored and good as new.
WHAT YOU NEED	(1) Two wooden matches. (2) An opaque man's handkerchief with a hem.
HOW IT WORKS	A match is previously inserted *into* the hem of a handkerchief so that it is completely concealed.

The second match is openly shown and apparently placed under the handker chief. In reality, you move the corner with the match in its hem under the hand kerchief and move it to the center.

Ask the spectator to hold the match. As he holds and feels the match that is in the hem, momentarily clip the other match between your right second and third fingers. Have the spectator break the one he is holding by snapping it in half.

Take the broken pieces between your left thumb and forefinger, squeezing them through the fabric. Eventually release the clipped corner and simultaneously place an end of the whole match between your left thumb and finger. Say, *"Now I want you to hold the match!"*

Transfer the handkerchief and whole match to the spectator, who is asked to hold it tightly in a similar grip. Say, *"You must utter the magic words, 'Amazing Cigar!' Did you feel something?"* Have the spectator check to find a restored match.

High-tech Version: This will puzzle anyone who knows the classic version. The extra match is not placed in the hem, but in your trouser pocket. The handker chief is then spread over your thigh. Rest the foot of this leg on the seat of a near by chair. The hidden match in your pocket should be just beneath the center of the draped handkerchief.

Show the other match and place it under the cloth, but have the spectator grasp and break the match in your pocket. Conclude as in the original version. The advantage in this method is the handkerchief can be borrowed and meticulous ly examined at the end.

High-tech Version #2: Conceal the duplicate match in the end of your necktie. You can now perform without wearing a coat or with your coat open. The hand kerchief is held close to your body. When you apparently place the match beneath the handkerchief, secretly bring the end of your tie underneath at the center and have the spectator grip the hidden match.

After the match is broken, say, *"Shake the hanky and holler 'heal'!"* When the handkerchief is shaken, your tie will drop down unnoticed and you are guilt-free. The whole match will fall to be examined.

AMAZING CIGAR FACTOID During the heyday of cigar production in America, there were 100,000 factories in the United States.

QUICK TURNAROUND

This is a complete swindle. You will immediately love it.

WHAT YOU SEE

You hold both hands into upright fists and ask your victim to place a match with its head pointing up into the top of one fist and another match with its head pointing down into the top of your other fist. Both matches are pushed into the fist. Without any further maneuvering or funny business, both hands are opened and the matches are shown to be pointing the *same direction*.

WHAT YOU NEED

Two wooden matches.

HOW IT WORKS

This is automatic. You do not do anything. Begin with the matches pointing in opposite directions. (Fig. 1) Push them down and into your fists with your thumbs. (Fig. 2)

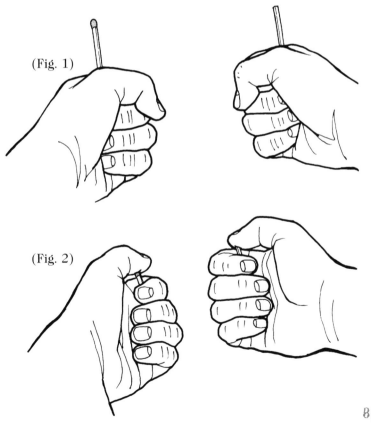

(Fig. 1)

(Fig. 2)

83

Tap your fists together, then immediately turn your hands palm up. (Fig. 3 Notice that the heads of the matches are pointing west and in the same direc tion. Let them roll off your fingertips and onto the table. Let your victim stare a only the matches. Because your hands are now out of play, it will be difficult fo anyone to reconstruct exactly how this happened.

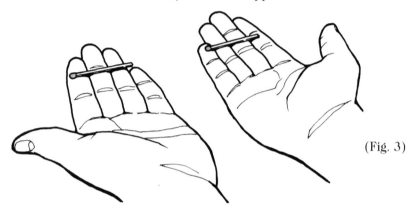

(Fig. 3)

JUMPY

This is a terrific routine.

WHAT YOU SEE	Two matches are placed on the table. One is placed in each hand, ye one of the matches jumps to the other hand. This is repeated a coupl of times, then you fool them a third time with a surprise twist.
WHAT YOU NEED	Two wooden matches.
HOW IT WORKS	A wooden match is placed on the table and your left hand is place palm up with your fingers pointing toward your victim. The matcl should be directly below these fingers. The second match is on the tabl to the right, head pointing away from you.

Pick up the second match with your right hand. The best way to hold the matcl is to take the head between your thumb and forefinger, the stem going back int your palm, and the back of your hand uppermost.

Pretend to place it into your left palm. As your left fingers curl inward to apparently take it, two things happen: (1) Your right hand retains the match between your thumb and forefinger; (2) The match that was hidden under your left fingers is exposed.

The second thing is important. The right-hand match is momentarily concealed by your curled left fingers. The only thing visible is the match made visible by the foregoing action. The victims are distracted by the appearance of the visible match and they are momentarily distracted at the right instant.

Your right hand picks up the visible match with your thumb and second finger. Do not try to palm the first match. Simply hold it in the same pick-up position. Maneuver both matches into your right hand, then wiggle both closed fists.

Open your left hand and show it empty, then open your right hand and let both matches roll onto the table. Repeat this for anyone slow on the uptake.

After you have performed this trick a couple of times, try this for a kicker finish. Place your left hand palm up and flat on the table. This time pretend to place a match under it and further back, but really retain it in your right hand.

Proceed as usual by picking up the match on the right with your right hand. As you place it in your left hand, leave *both* matches there. As your left fingers close and your left hand raises and moves slightly to the left, reach down to pick up the match supposedly on the table. Look surprised when you see that it is not there. Open your left hand and roll out both matches. This is "gotcha" number two.

AMAZING CIGAR FACTOID

A North Carolina man bought several expensive cigars and insured them against—get this!—fire. After he smoked them all, he then decided to submit a claim against the insurance company. The insurance company refused to pay, citing the obvious reason that the man had consumed the cigars in a normal fashion. The man sued. The judge stated that since the company had insured the cigars against fire, they were obligated to pay. After the man accepted payment for his claim, the insurance company had the man arrested...for committing arson.

PIANO MOVER

This swindle is nine days older than water, but magicians and con men are still exploiting its underlying principle.

Someone places his hands palms down on the table as though he or sh were playing an imaginary piano. You remove fifteen matches from matchbox and place them between your victim's fingers. (Fig. 1) Th matches are placed in pairs except for one.

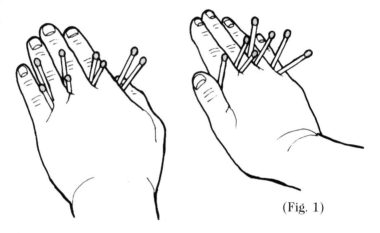

(Fig. 1)

One at a time these pairs of matches are removed and separated into tw groups, one match being placed to the left and the other to the righ When you have finished separating the pairs into two groups on th table, point to the odd one still left in the victim's hand.

You ask the victim to point to a pile. You explain that you will put th "odd" match into the chosen pile, which you subsequently do. After a li tle verbal mumbo-jumbo, you say that the "odd" match has traveled the other pile. You further explain that since the matches were in pair you will recount them in the same fashion.

You pick up the pile with the "odd" match and count matches two at time, each time saying, *"Two matches, even."* After you count fou "pairs" (even), add: *"It looks as though the 'odd' match has traveled the other pile."* Pick up the other pile and repeat the counting of pair You will count three "pairs" (even) and will be left with one (odd) matc

86

AT YOU EED

Fifteen wooden matches.

OW WORKS

The secret to this sweet swindle lies in the fact that you separated seven pairs of matches into two groups. Each pile actually consisted of *seven* matches, an odd number. Adding the extra match makes the pile even.

Do not feel too guilty about the boldness of this swindle. Quickly pick up the matches and replace them in the box before anyone thinks too deeply about what really happened.

AMAZING CIGAR
QUOTE

"Sometimes a cigar is just a cigar."
— *Sigmund Freud*

TESTOSTERONE LEVEL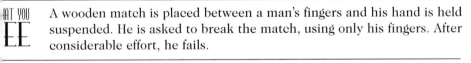

This is a guy thing.

AT YOU EE

A wooden match is placed between a man's fingers and his hand is held suspended. He is asked to break the match, using only his fingers. After considerable effort, he fails.

AT YOU EED

A wooden match.

OW WORKS

Have a man hold a wooden match so that its center rests on top of his middle finger and below the first joints of his first and third fingers. Emphasize that the fingers must be kept straight throughout the exertion. His hand must be held in the air, not against a flat surface or table. It looks easy, but a match held in this position is difficult to break using only the strength of the fingers.

FLEA CIRCUS

This uses the same tricky move explained in "Jumpy."

WHAT YOU SEE
Using a couple of paper matches, you simulate a flea circus where tir fleas apparently jump around and perform acrobatic tricks.

WHAT YOU NEED
(1) Two paper matches. (2) A pen.

HOW IT WORKS
Using the pen, draw two solid bug-like dots on one side of a match nea its head and leave the other side blank. This is designated Match A Draw one dot in the same place on the other match, leaving the othe side blank. This is designated Match B.

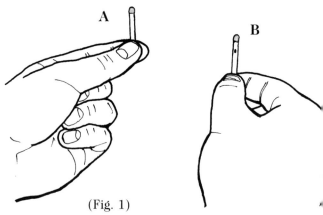

Hold the double-dotted Match A with its blank-side showing between your *left* thumb and first finger. Hold the other match with its single-dot side showing in the same manner between your right thumb and first finger. (Fig. 1)

(Fig. 1)

The entire illusion consists of secretly turning the matches over by rotating thei edges between your thumbs and forefingers. You may rotate the match clockwis or counter-clockwise, depending on which comes easier to you. Simply pinc and move your thumbs and forefingers in opposite directions. The match wil instantly flip over. This smaller action will be covered by a larger action—b either by moving your hand up and down or back and forth.

Show both matches and ask, *"Have you ever seen a flea circus?"* Regardless o your friend's answer, say: *"Notice my flea."* Extend your right hand and show th single dot on top of Match B. (Fig. 1)

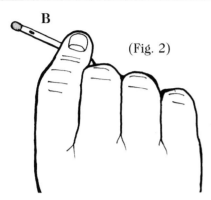

(Fig. 2)

Continue: *"I know there's another flea around here!"* Perform the flip-over move as you turn your right hand palm down, ostensibly to show the other side of Match B. (Fig. 2) In reality, you are showing the same single-dot side. Say, *"Oh! There he is!"* Your friend will assume that the second "flea" simply appeared on the other side.

Turn your right hand palm up again and reverse the process so that the single-dot side is back on top. Say, *"Let's see if the flea underneath and the one on top can jump to the other match!"* Move both the right-hand (B) and left-hand (A) matches forward in a quick jerking action and perform the secret flip-over with each match. Two "fleas" will instantly appear on top of the left-hand (A) match and the right-hand (B) match will appear blank. (Fig. 3)

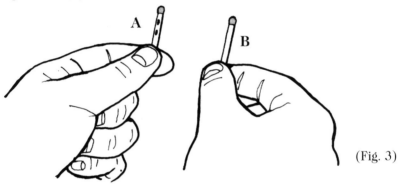

(Fig. 3)

Perform the flip-over move again as you quickly move the left-hand Match A up and down. Say, *"Where did they go?"* This time, move your right-hand match (B) up and down in a quick action and simultaneously perform the flip-over move. A "flea" will appear on top. Perform the turnover and flip-over move to apparently show the other side, adding: *"Oh, yeah...There's the other critter!"*

Say, *"Sometimes one jumps away."* Make a gesture with the right-hand (B) match, then show the other (blank) side. Hand this match to your friend for examination and place Match A in your pocket.

As you can see, all kinds of combinations are possible. How droll and cute do you want to be? You can make "fleas" disappear, jump, multiply to your heart's content. Once you have mastered the flip-over move, you can perform this cute stunt as long as there are two matches and a pen.

Use your acting ability. It helps to move your head and eyes back and forth as you seem to follow the movement of the performing fleas.

89

MATCHBOX
BAMBOOZLERS

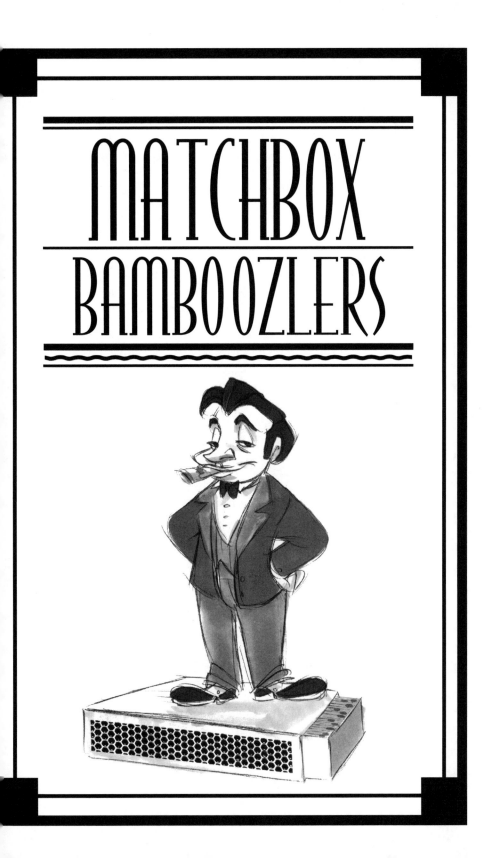

RATTLING MONTE

The ancient three-shell game and three-card Monte are notorious cons, which are still foisted on unsuspecting dupes. This variant does not require any skill or extra gimmickry. Everything seems fair and aboveboard, yet the game is rigged in a devious way.

WHAT YOU SEE

Three empty matchboxes are shown and a quarter is placed inside of one of the boxes. The game is to keep track of the box with the coin as they are moved around the table. The victim never wins.

WHAT YOU NEED

(1) Four wooden matchboxes. (2) Two quarters. Each quarter is placed into a box so that it will rattle when shaken. The other two are empty.

HOW IT WORKS

Place one of the matchboxes with a coin inside into the cuff of your left shirtsleeve. If you wear a watch with an expansion band, tuck it under the band. You will now fool your victim by "sound" instead of tricky sleight of hand.

Show the three matchboxes. Dump out the quarter and let your victim examine everything. Place the quarter into one of the boxes and close the drawers of all three. Place the one with the quarter in the middle of the other two. Say, "Your job is to keep your eye on the box with the quarter inside it."

Pick up the center box with your *right* hand and shake it so that the quarter rattles. Switch the boxes around several times, then ask your victim to point to the one with the quarter inside. Regardless of which one he chooses, pick up another box with your *left* hand and shake it. Your victim will hear the rattle of the quarter in the *sleeved* box. Say, "You must have blinked or something. I'll move the boxes much slower this time."

Your victim will now closely watch an *empty* box. Move the boxes around slowly. Keep track of the one you know has the quarter inside. Ask your victim to point to a box. When he points to the wrong one, point to the right one and have him pick it up and shake it. Have him open the box to check.

You can repeat this swindle as often as you like or until your victim weakens and begs for mercy. If you are a betting person, you can bet a box of cigars. In the end, don't take them but offer your victim your best cigar for being a good sport. After all, you have had your fun.

JPSY DAISY

his swindle will have your analytical friends scratching their heads.

HAT YOU
SEE

You hand someone a box of wooden matches that is identical to yours. You both start out with boxes rightside up. You explain a game of You-Do-As-I-Do, where your friend must emulate all of your actions. After a series of turnovers, your box ends rightside up and his box is upside down. This is repeated several times.

WHAT YOU
NEED

(1) Two identical matchboxes. (2) An Exacto knife or razor blade.

HOW
WORKS

Take one of the matchboxes and remove the drawer from its cover and shell. Dump out the matches. Cut the drawer exactly in half with the Exacto knife. If a knife is not available, you can carefully rip the box in half. Insert one of the half-drawers rightside up into the right side of the shell and place the other half-drawer upside down into the left side of the shell. (Fig. 1: The dark lines in the schematic drawing represent the solid parts of the drawer as viewed from the side.)

(Fig. 1)

f you leave the drawers sticking out part way, the resultant condition should look like Figure 2. Replace the matches, but when you replace them put half of he matches with their heads facing one direction and the other half facing the opposite direction. You now have a matchbox that serves the same purpose as a double-headed coin. This box, henceforth, is known as the faked box.

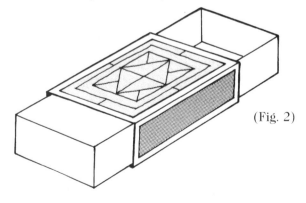

(Fig. 2)

93

Introduce both boxes and hand the regular box to your victim. Ask, *"Have you ever heard of the game called You-Do-As-I-Do?"* When the victim shrugs, add *"All you have to do is watch closely and duplicate my exact actions. Pay attention. Don't blink. Don't get distracted!"*

Open your drawer so that the end that is rightside up appears and the matches can be seen. You must be able to identify this end. Let the spectator fumble around until he gets his matchbox correctly arranged. Say, *"Our drawers are rightside up."*

Close your drawer and turn the box *sideways*. Let the victim perform the same action. Turn the box over *endwise*. Let the victim imitate. Turn yours *sideways* again and let the spectator imitate.

Open your drawer the correct way and remove a match. The victim's drawer will be upside down. Say, *"Oops! You must have done something different. You see it starts out rightside up, then goes rightside down, then end-over-end, upsy daisy, then upside and rightside down, then it ends up right! Got it?"*

Repeat the sequence until the victim has a crisis of self-confidence, then say *"Never mind. Have a cigar on me?"* Hand him a cigar, wait a couple of seconds then add, *"Need me to light it?"*

GHOSTLY MATCHBOX

This requires some time-consuming preparation, but the ultimate effect is worth going the extra mile. It will astound your fellow smokers!

WHAT YOU SEE	You show a matchbox, which becomes animated in a ghostly manner. It slides and the drawer full of matches opens of its own accord. It seems to have a will of its own.
WHAT YOU NEED	(1) A wooden matchbox with a sliding drawer or tray. (2) A length of invisible nylon thread 10 inches long that can be purchased from a fabric store or nylon fishing line. (3) A small safety pin. (4) A sewing needle.
HOW IT WORKS	Remove the drawer from the matchbox and punch a couple of holes in the top of the matchbox *shell*. The distance between the holes should be about an eighth of an inch. Punch a pair of identical and corresponding holes in the bottom of the *drawer*. Thread the needle with the nylon thread, then push the threaded needle through the hole (X) near the rear of the box. Tie a knot on the loose end and push the needle through the hole. Move the thread over the top of the shell and toward its front, then move it down to the rear of the second (bottom) hole and *up* through it. (Figs. 1 and 2)

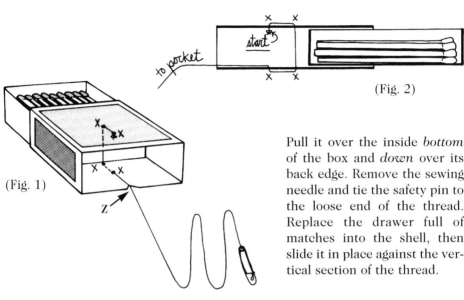

(Fig. 2)

(Fig. 1)

Pull it over the inside *bottom* of the box and *down* over its back edge. Remove the sewing needle and tie the safety pin to the loose end of the thread. Replace the drawer full of matches into the shell, then slide it in place against the vertical section of the thread.

Cut a tiny slit into the matchbox shell marked Z and slide the thread through it to stabilize and center it. Affix the safety pin to the *inside* of your right jacket pocket. Place the matchbox in this pocket and you are ready to go.

This is less tricky than it reads. Now that you have gone the extra mile, a little practice with the props will make everything familiar and easy to understand.

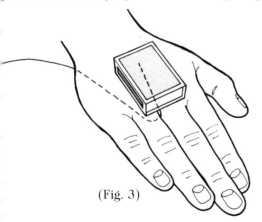

(Fig. 3)

Remove the closed matchbox from your right coat pocket and maneuver the thread *between* your right second and third fingers. Use your left hand to place the box onto your palm-down right hand. (Fig. 3) Ask, *"Have you ever used these kind of matches? Take a good look at the box."* At this stage the thread cannot be seen.

Keep your right hand *stationary*. You will be able to make the box move in a ghostly fashion by imperceptibly moving your *body*. You must put tension on the anchored thread. By slightly moving your body backwards and away from your right hand, the matchbox will move *forward* on your hand. This immediately focuses attention on the box. Say, *"Spooky, huh! It's called the Poltergeist Effect!*

Grasp the matchbox with your right hand and openly slide it back to its original position. Repeat the "ghostly" movement. Now grasp the box with your left hand and slide it to the extreme tips of your right second and third fingers.

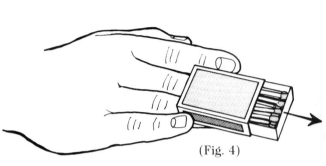

(Fig. 4)

Your right first and pinky fingers clip the sides of the box. Hold the box tightly and move your body backwards. The taut thread, still hidden under your fingers, will cause the drawer to slide open. (Fig. 4)

Slide the drawer back into place with your left hand and add, *"I hate it when that happens!"* Slide the front end of the box toward the back of your right hand. In the process, turn it over so that the thread is on top of the box and say, *"Look at what happens when I do this!"*

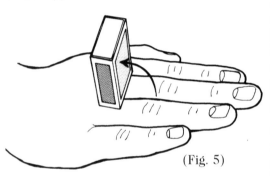

(Fig. 5)

A slight secret movement will cause the box to lever upright on its end. (Fig. 5) Turn the box end-for-end so that its upper end rests on your right second and third fingers and is again clipped between your forefinger and pinky. Say, *"When the moon is right, it does this!"* Make another slight body movement and the drawer will slide out and *upward.* (Fig. 6) This is a killer finish.

If you like, cover the matchbox with an inverted clear drinking glass prior to the climactic drawer-rise. This may be gilding the lily, but the option is possible. Afterwards, close the box and place it back in your pocket. If you have an unprepared, duplicate matchbox in your pocket, let your victim fully respond to the weirdness he has just seen and then remove the ordinary box. Hand it to him, saying: *"Perhaps you want to take this home? If so, I cannot be responsible for what happens."*

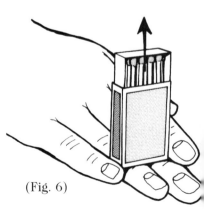

(Fig. 6)

FORKLIFT U

This is a dexterity teaser. It looks like an easy maneuver to do, but when your victim tries it, he will feel uncoordinated and feeble.

WHAT YOU SEE

You place a matchbox on the table in front of a shot glass. The apparently simple task is to place your palm-down right hand in back of the matchbox with your second and third finger*tips* firmly anchored against the tabletop. Your first and fourth fingers straddle the ends of the matchbox.

Now using only your first and fourth fingers and without lifting your other fingertips off the table, you must lift the box onto the *top* of the shot glass.

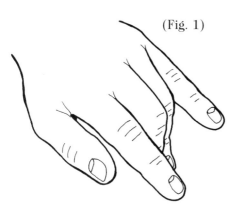

(Fig. 1)

Place a matchbox on the table in front of a shot glass. Place your second and third fingertips against the table with your first and fourth fingers extended. (Fig. 1) Say, "*I want you to place your hand on the table like this. You must keep the tips of your second and third fingers against the table at all times. Can you move your first and fourth fingers up and down?*"

Move your first and fourth fingers up and down like the blades of a forklift. Most spectators will be able to emulate these actions. This will falsely build their confidence. After they have practiced the action a few times, position your right hand behind the matchbox. Your first and fourth fingers *straddle the ends* of the matchbox. (Fig. 2) Position the upside-down shot glass in front of the matchbox.

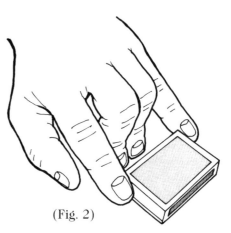

(Fig. 2)

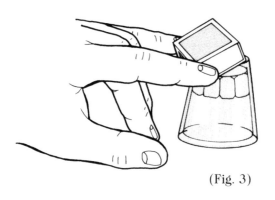

(Fig. 3)

Say, *"The simple task is to place your palm-down right hand in back of the matchbox with your second and third fingertips firmly anchored against the table top, then by using only your first and fourth fingers and without lifting your other fingertips off the table, lift the matchbox onto the top of the shot glass."* (Fig. 3)

WHAT YOU NEED

(1) A couple of matchboxes. (2) A shot glass.

HOW IT WORKS

Practice. This is not the answer you want to read. We wish there were an arcane, easy solution. Some people are able to instantly perform this maneuver. Others flounder and feel completely uncoordinated. They eventually give up, even though it looks like child's play.

If you really want to taunt your victim, when you demonstrate the maneuver, do it in two steps, using the other matchbox instead of a shot glass. Put the other matchbox so that it is flat and in front of the primary matchbox. Perform the maneuver and place the primary matchbox on top of the second matchbox. Say, *"Understand the game? It is easy."*

Remove the primary matchbox, then turn the second matchbox on its end. Repeat the maneuver, this time placing the primary matchbox on top of the higher elevation. Say, *"This is a bit harder!"* Needless to say, your victim will probably stumble at the initial challenge.

Practice this one. You will be surprised. If your victim likes to wager, you can win a few drinks with this one.

AMAZING CIGAR FACTOID

Johnny "Cigar" Connors smoked 600 cigars in 48 hours in Roxbury, MA on February 25, 1933. He did not eat or drink during this marathon smoke-fest.

TUNNEL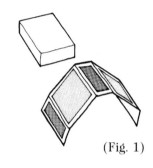

Enduring puzzles are distinguished by the utter simplicity of the props and conditions, coupled with the ingeniousness of their solutions. This one fits this special category.

WHAT YOU SEE

You introduce a matchbox and convert the shell into a makeshift *tunnel*. The empty drawer is placed on the far side of the "tunnel." (Fig. 1) You tell your victim that his goal is to get the drawer to travel under and through the "tunnel" so that it rests on the other or near side. He or she may not touch the tray or "tunnel" with anything. No other props or objects can be used.

(Fig. 1)

WHAT YOU NEED

A matchbox.

HOW IT WORKS

Place your left hand in *back* of the tray as you face the "tunnel" and tray. Hold your hand flat, fingers together, to form a "wall."

Take a deep breath and robustly blow against your hand. (Fig. 2) The deflecting "gust" will propel the drawer through the "tunnel" and toward you. (Fig. 3)

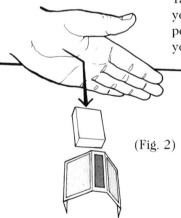

(Fig. 2)

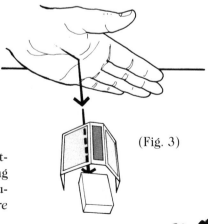

(Fig. 3)

If you are inclined to soften this unexpected "blow" to your victim's ego, assuming that he or she failed to discover the solution, simply smile and add, *"There are advantages to being a blowhard!"*

99

VAN DEVENTER'S MASTERPIECE

Here's a cross between a puzzle and modern art. We love this one.

WHAT YOU SEE

It is one of the most ingenious puzzles we have ever seen. Although it uses only five simple matchboxes, it is a real challenge to create the final product. The structure, by the way, makes an eye-arresting desk sculpture and conversation piece. When someone asks about it, take it apart to show its five components and then say, *"Put them back together again. All you have to do is close all the boxes. In other words, all five drawers must be slid into an adjoining cover or sleeve."* This looks fairly straightforward at first blush, but the puzzle-solver will soon find himself up against a formidable engineering problem.

The completed structure looks like Figure 1.

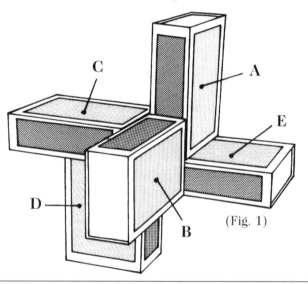

(Fig. 1)

WHAT YOU NEED

(1) Five sturdy matchboxes. Most standard matchboxes have the correct proportion, but make certain that the length-width-height proportions are 3:2:1. (2) Strong paper-cardboard adhesive.

HOW IT WORKS

First you will need to do some construction with the matchboxes. Glue the drawer or tray to its respective shell or cover in accordance with Figure 2, which designates the five separate matchboxes as A, B, C, D and E. They must be precisely glued together as shown.

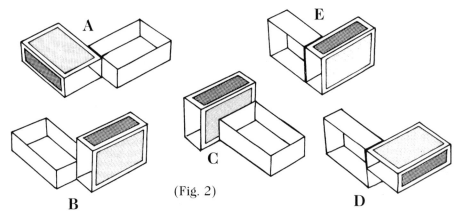

A

E

B

C

(Fig. 2)

D

f you want to challenge yourself, try to solve the puzzle without looking at the
olution. There are *three* known solutions. Here is one of them: Put A and B
ogether. C goes onto the A-B unit, then D goes into E. Put D and E as a unit to
nit A, B, and C. (Fig. 3)

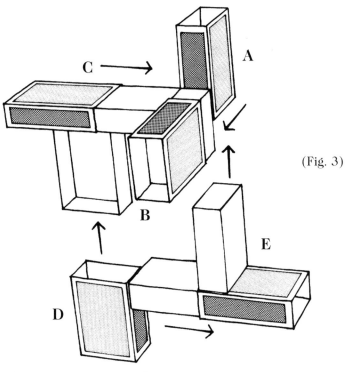

C ⟶   A

(Fig. 3)

B

E

D

MIND GAMES

Giovanni handed Racherbaumer a piece of paper. It read: **Now will you please read this sentence carefully.**
Racherbaumer did.

"*Now what?*" Racherbaumer asked.

"*How many times does the letter E appear?*"

Racherbaumer looked again and grinned. "*Oh, yeah, I see what you mean. Many people will overlook the e's at the end of 'please' and 'sentence.' There are actually seven e's. It's like magic. People don't notice what's plainly visible.*"

The puzzles in our Mind Games section are like this. The solution may be hidden in plain sight, although it's your mind's eye that must see it. Though we call these mental challenges Mind Games, some call them brainteasers or bar bets—puzzles frequently formulated as wagers. Most use commonplace items usually carried on your person or found in a bar: matches, glasses, napkins, cigars straws, pencils. We chose something cigar smokers always have on hand—wooden matches.

Such challenges, at first glance, look starkly simple, almost childish. Yet when you sit down to play, the situation quickly changes. The puzzle is harder than it looks. This is the mark of a great puzzle. Its solution is simple but subtle—so simple, in fact, that you kick yourself in the head and shout, "*But of course!*" No matter. Your sense of victimization will immediately disappear when you contemplate your next victim.

Mind Games are also double-edged in a devilish way. If you immediately solve the puzzle, you feel exhilaration and a sense of relief. If you fail miserably, you are not alone. Most people cannot solve puzzles of great impenetrability. So, everybody gets an A for trying. After all, even Einstein failed math. The whole idea is to exercise your brain and have fun. When you show your friends the same puzzles and they flounder and whine, you can always say, "*Yeah...that one's a toughie. It took me almost twenty seconds to get it!*"

Ever since the days of the great Sam Lloyd (one of the greatest puzzle-makers of this century), brainteasers, puzzles, and mind games have challenged problem-solvers of all ages. Puzzles using lighters and matches are particularly ingenious because the props are innocent looking and commonplace.

We have chosen some of the best, most enduring puzzles based on simple criteria: The conditions and nature of the problem are easy to understand and must look, at first blush, easy to solve. Also, the solution must be ingenious, cute, or an absolute cheat.

These puzzles are great fun for patrons of cigar parlors, barroom customers, or cocktail party guests. If you have a box of wooden matches, you are in business. Try your hand at each puzzle before checking the solutions at the back of this book, then try them out at your next party or informal gathering. Your mother always told you never to play with matches...it's time to break the rules!

OLIVE FOIL

Place four matches into the configuration shown. These matches represent a Martini glass. The fifth object is a broken match head, which is placed inside the glass.

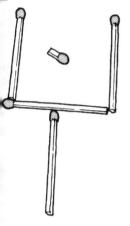

The challenge is to move and reposition only two full-sized matches so that the match-head is outside the glass.

To mislead your victim and start him thinking in the wrong direction, show him an incorrect or unsuccessful solution. Move the match composing the "stem" and reposition it at the top to momentarily form a square. Then take the bottom side of the square and reposition it as a "stem" at the top. This results in forming an upside down glass, but the match-head is still inside it. Say, *"As you can see, the olive is still in the glass. This is an example of a wrong solution!"*

Solution on p. 141

SQUARES GONE

Move and reposition three matches to transform seven squares into five squares.

Solution on p. 141

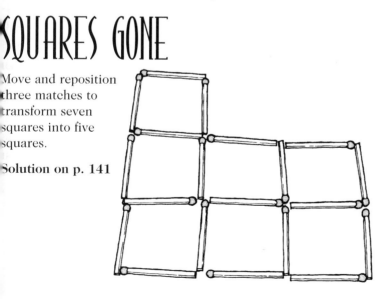

FIVE TO FOUR

There are five squares. Move and reposition two matches to form four squares.

Solution on p. 142

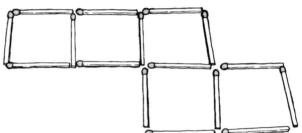

MENSA BASH

These sixteen matches form two squares, a smaller one inside a large one. Move and reposition only four matches to make three squares.

Solution on p. 142

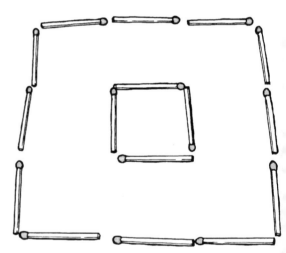

TRIANGULATION

These nine matches form three triangles. Move and reposition two to form four triangles.

Solution on p. 142

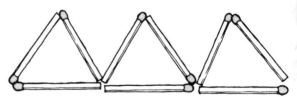

108

TRIANGULATION OUTDONE

This one seems impossible. You start with two triangles. Using only these matches, reposition them to form *four* triangles.

Hint: All four are the same size as the original triangles.

Solution on p. 143

MAKE IT EQUAL

Without touching any of the matches, make this equation equal.

Solution on p. 143

STARLET

Without touching the matches with your person, make these matches into a star.

Solution on p. 144

ROOT OF IT

Move only one match and reposition it to make this formula equal.

Solution on p. 144

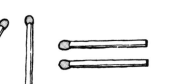

NINNEY

Add these six matches to the other five to obtain nine.

Solution on p. 144

EDGY

Can you drop a paper match so that it lands on its edge?

Solution on p. 144

NIM

This ancient strategy game became popular when it appeared in an art film from the 60s called *Last Year At Marienbad*. Three rows of wooden matches are placed on the table. Each row has a different number of matches in it. Two players take alternate turns. A turn consists of removing as many matches as one wishes— from one to all—from a given row. The object of the game is to *not* be left with only one match.

Solution on p. 144

ABOUT-FACE FISH

Move and reposition only two matches and make the fish look like it is swimming in the opposite direction.

Solution on p. 145

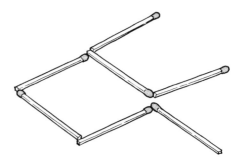

FLYING SOUTH

Move and reposition three match-es so that the formation of the birds changes from flying north to flying south.

Solution on p. 145

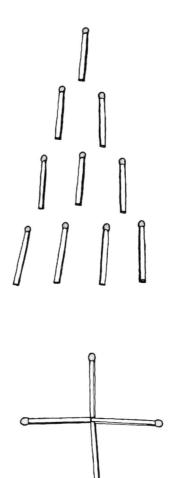

PERFECT SQUARE

Move only one match to form a perfect square.

Solution on p. 146

LIGHTER SIDE

PINOCCHIO KNOWS

Raymond Smullyan, a professor of mathematical logic and a performing magician, is the king of logical puzzles. A writer of many books on the subject, including *What Is The Name Of This Book?*, he is someone who knows how to entertain with the deepest paradoxes of logic and set theory. How can you resist someone who writes, "Which is better, eternal happiness or a ham sandwich? It would appear that eternal happiness is better, but this is really not so! After all, nothing is better than eternal happiness, and a ham sandwich is better than nothing. Therefore, a ham sandwich is better than eternal happiness."

This application of Smullyan-type logic comes from Gerald Kosky and Barrie Richardson.

WHAT YOU SEE

You invite two spectators to assist and hand them your lighter. The spectators decide which one will keep the lighter. The lighter is hidden in the hand. Next they decide which one will be a fibber. The other must always tell the truth. You, by the way, do not know which one has the lighter and which one is the designated fibber. You ask one of the spectators only one question: *"Does the liar have the lighter?"* The spectator, depending on his role as truth-teller or fibber, replies yes or no. Regardless, you instantly know which one has the lighter.

WHAT YOU NEED

A lighter.

HOW IT WORKS

This is based on logic, but the logic is obscured. Pay attention. Here goes: If the designated liar has the lighter, he must answer no. If he does *not* have the lighter, he must answer yes. If the designated truth-teller has the lighter, he will answer no. If he does not have it, he will answer yes. There are only four possible scenarios, yet you can always discern who has the lighter, regardless of whom you ask.

If the person you ask says no, he is holding the lighter. If the person says yes, he is *not* holding the lighter. At first blush, this may seem confusing, but if you analyze everything, it becomes obvious. If you want a memory aid, remember the word Zippo (the name of a lighter). In slang terminology, "zip" means "nothing" which connects you to "no." If the spectator says no, he has the lighter.

If you want to get fancy and involve three women, use Barrie Richardson's sophisticated approach. He uses *three* objects instead of one.

Invite three cigar-smoking ladies to assist. Have each one designate one of their hands as being either a fibber or truth-teller. Introduce a lighter, a coin, and a cigar band from your favorite cigar. Say, *"We are going to perform an experiment which requires total concentration. Brain researchers tell us that our hands and their activities are connected to the opposite hemispheres of the brain. I want each of you to pretend that your two hands are two separate persons. I want you to designate one hand to be a complete, unrepentant liar. Your other hand will be a forthright truth-teller.*

Make certain that the ladies understand the premise. Continue: *"If I ask one of your hands a question, you must answer that question based on the character of that hand. For example, if I asked the hand that fibs, 'Are you a liar?' you would answer 'no' because that hand always fibs. Your other hand would never lie."*

Hand out the three objects, one to each lady, then have each lady *mentally* designate her hands accordingly. Ask them to place their hands behind their backs. Have each hold her object in one hand, then form both hands into fists. Say, *"Please hold your closed fists in front of your body. Are you sure which hand is which? Make certain you know which tells the truth and which lies. Finally, decide which hand is going to be the spokesperson."*

Address the lady that has the lighter: *"Hold up your spokesperson-hand. Only you know whether or not this hand is a fibber or truth-teller. Only you know which hand holds the lighter. I'm going to ask you one question. Please answer according to the character of the hand you're holding up. If it's a liar, tell a lie. If it's a truth-teller, tell the truth. Think carefully before you reply!"* Ask, *"Does your liar-hand hold the lighter?"* If she replies no, tap her raised hand and say, *"This hand holds the lighter."* If she replies yes, tap the other hand.

Address the second lady who holds the coin, but alter the question: *"Does your truth-teller hand have the coin?"* This reverses the outcome. The fellow smokers will be confused because the wording is changed. They are also entertaining the mistaken idea that you are trying to find out two things: which hand is a fibber or truth-teller and which one is holding the coin. This is too much information to obtain by a single question. To make matters more perplexing, you respond differently the second time.

Move quickly to the third lady holding the cigar band and say, *"This time, I'll choose which of your hands will be the spokesperson.* Touch her left hand, have her hold it up, and say, *"Only you know whether or not this hand is a liar or truth-teller. Isn't that so? Well, does the liar-hand have the cigar band?"* Depending on her response, tap the correct hand.

It is important to *carefully* explain the premise at the outset. Using three people and dealing with them in *quick succession* creates a strong impression. It also overcomes the even-money aspects of the proposition. Do not pass up this quickie. After you try it a few times, it is easy to do and remember. Fellow smokers will remember the premise and your apparent divination ability.

ASBESTOS HANDKERCHIEF

Turn a normal handkerchief into a superhero's cape. This must be seen to be believed.

WHAT YOU SEE	You remove a white pocket handkerchief and have two spectators each hold two adjacent corners so that the handkerchief can be held taut and flat. You remove a lighter, ignite it, and pass it *under* the handkerchief. The flame, however, remains burning *above* the cloth, following the zigzag path of the lighter. When the lighter is finally removed and extinguished, the handkerchief is shown to be *whole* rather than hole-y.
WHAT YOU NEED	(1) A white handkerchief. (2) A Zippo or Bic lighter. (3) Caution.
HOW IT WORKS	The only trick to this stunt is to keep the lighter moving. After you ignite it, move the flaming wick to the nearest hem of the handkerchief. Pass the lighter underneath and push it against the underside of the cloth. Keep it moving in a zigzag path. The flame will burn above the cloth because the vapor filters through the cloth.

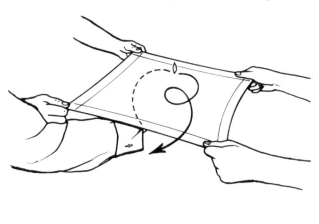

You do not have to move the lighter too fast—just fast enough to prevent any damage. Remove and extinguish the lighter, then pass out the handkerchief for examination. If you have the nerve, borrow the handkerchief. This is not for the faint-hearted. Use caution and common sense. Fire burns.

COUNTDOWN CON

The ancestry of this stunt is unknown. Giovanni says, "Remember the put-down about walking and chewing gum at the same time? This stunt is like that. Trying to do two things simultaneously, depending on what they are, is often difficult. This stunt demonstrates the importance of *listening carefully* and watching closely. If you miss a critical detail, you cannot succeed. Once your brain locks up, you will not overcome the initial block."

WHAT YOU SEE

Three cigar lighters are lined in a row on the table. A spectator is cautioned to pay close attention. You count backwards from ten, using a special procedure as the lighters are picked up and replaced in succession. The goal is to repeat the identical actions, along with the accompanying words, and end up with all three lighters on the table. Although the procedure is simple, the spectator stumbles and cannot meet the challenge.

WHAT YOU NEED

Three cigar lighters.

HOW IT WORKS

Place the lighters in a row on the table. Address the spectator: *"It is very important to listen to what I say and watch what I do."* Pick up one of the lighters at an end of the row and say, *"Ten..."* Pick up the next two in succession, adding, *"...nine...eight..."*

Replace two on the table in a row and in succession, saying, *"...seven...six..."* Show the remaining lighter in your hand and say, *"...one in the hand..."* Pick up the two tabled lighters again in succession, adding: *"...five...four..."*

Replace all three back on the table in succession, saying: *"...three...two...one!"* Explain that all three lighters must end up on the table and the pick-ups and put-downs must be made in *unison* with the actions.

Pick up the lighters and repeat the same dialogue without using the lighters. *The next move is critical.* Hand your victim the lighters and immediately say, *"Remember! Start out by saying, 'Ten, nine, eight...' Just like they do at NASA!"*

At this point, the spectator will concentrate on what to say, not realizing that he is starting with the lighters *in his hand*, not on the table. *He is starting out wrong!* When he gets to "six" in his countdown, he will suddenly stop because he will have *two* lighters in his hand and the patter indicates that he should have only one (*"one in the hand"*).

Take the lighters out of his hand, place them on the table in a row, and say, *"It looks like the one-in-the-hand part is throwing you. Remember, the countdown is backwards."* Repeat the correct action and patter. Over-emphasize the one-in-the-hand bit when you come to it, then pick up the lighters and gently ask, *"Got it?"*

Hand him the lighters. As long as he takes them *in hand*, he is out of luck. If he places the lighters on the table to start, you are busted. Game over. Some people are quick studies and immediately duplicate the words and actions. Most people, however, stumble a few times before they figure out the sting. This is a lot of fun.

CUTTER CUNNING

LOOPY

If you do not extricate the cutter right away, you will fumble around for hours.

WHAT YOU SEE
You have just cut the end of your cigar with your elegant cutter, whic you have on a loop of cord around your neck. You slyly look at yo cigar-smoking friend and say, *"I see you noticed that my cutter is wor around my neck."* You remove the loop and place it around your friend neck, saying: *"Notice that it is not exactly tied on the cutter. It is loope in case I want to remove it completely. Your mission, should yo decide to accept it, is to remove the cutter without removing the loo from your neck or by breaking or cutting the cord."* Although some wi eventually discover how to disentangle the cutter, this is really a pre liminary to "Gordian Nightmare," a follow-up puzzle to bedevil an brain trust.

WHAT YOU NEED
(1) A scissors-type cigar cutter. (2) A two-foot length of cord.

HOW IT WORKS
Find the center of the cord then place this loop through one of the cut ter's finger-openings. You are going to form a Bridle Hitch, a form o knot used by cowboys to hitch reins to a hitching post. Once this cen ter loop is through the finger-opening, thread the two loose end; through the loop to form the "hitch," then tie the loose ends together (Fig. 1)

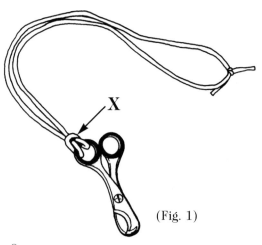

After uttering your preliminary remarks, remove the loop from around your neck and place it around your victim's neck so that the cutter hangs down in front of him. Explain the challenge, then watch him struggle.

X

(Fig. 1)

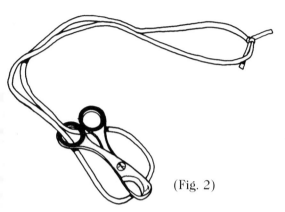

This is the simple solution. You must pull the loop marked X in Figure 1. Loosen and enlarge it so that you can pass it around the cutter in the correct direction as shown in Figure 2. This solution will eventually dawn on most people, but you want your victim's ego to inflate a bit. When his ego balloons, take back the cutter and cord and set up the next puzzle called the "Gordian Nightmare."

(Fig. 2)

GORDIAN NIGHTMARE

This will drive you nuts.

WHAT YOU SEE

This is a vexing follow-up to "Loopy."

WHAT YOU NEED

(1) A scissors-type cigar cutter. (2) A two-foot length of cord.

HOW IT WORKS

Find the center of the cord then place this loop through one of the cutter's finger-openings. You are going to form a Bridle Hitch again. Once this center loop is through the finger opening, thread the two loose ends through the loop to form the "hitch." So far it is exactly like the preparation for "Loopy." Before you tie the loose ends together, however, thread them through the *other* finger opening of the handle. (Fig. 1)

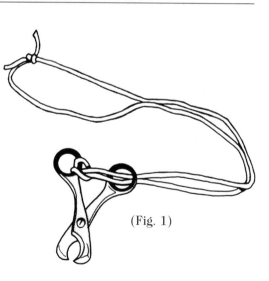

(Fig. 1)

Since your victim may have solved "Loopy," he is a prime candidate to be stymied. The puzzle does not look too problematical at first blush. Nevertheless, it will drive most people crazy.

Since we have a mild sadistic streak, a solution is not provided. Consider it a test of your tenacity, patience, and sanity. If you prefer, forget about solving this puzzle yourself. Foist it on your best friend. When he fails and begs you to show him the solution, smile and say, *"I could tell you, but that's no fun!"* If he does not beat you over the head with the cutter, admit that you don't know the answer, then run for the nearest exit.

Just kidding!

Solution on p. 146

AMAZING CIGAR FACTOID

If you think that being rebuffed or exiled from your favorite bar or restaurant because of your love of cigar smoking is bad, be grateful you didn't live in Turkey during the reign of Sultan Murad IV, who punished smokers by cutting off their noses.

FOLLOW CHEFALO

This is based on an interesting type of slipknot ascribed to an Italian magician named Chefalo.

WHAT YOU SEE

A rope is threaded through an opening in the handle of a cutter, then two knots are formed. Using only one end of the rope, thread through both knot-loops and the opening of the cutter to form a godawful entanglement. The ends are pulled tight and the cutter comes free. Efforts to duplicate this feat by others lead to Gordian-type knotting.

WHAT YOU NEED

(1) A scissors-type cigar cutter. (2) A two-foot length of cord.

HOW IT WORKS

Place the cutter on the center of the rope, then tie a single overhand knot. This means that the left end loops over the other end, then loops under. If you were a Boy Scout or in the Navy, you know the importance of being knot-savvy.

The second knot is just the opposite. Look closely at Fig. 1. If you do not make the two knots in this fashion, the final result will be unrewarding.

The next action follows the arrows. The end marked X in the drawing must follow the diagram. This is the only way the cutter can be freed when the ends are tightened. Most people who try to duplicate this feat will tie another overhand knot.

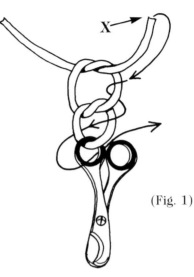

(Fig. 1)

IMPOSSIBLE KNOT

You will love the audacity of this one.

WHAT YOU SEE — You thread the handle of your cigar cutter onto the center of a rope, which you hold with both hands near the respective ends. Someone covers the rope and cutter with a handkerchief, then two spectators each hold an end of the rope. After some secret maneuverings under the handkerchief, you whisk it away to show that the cutter is now hanging from a knot in the rope—a topological impossibility!

WHAT YOU NEED — (1) A scissors-type cigar cutter. (2) A two-foot length of cord. (3) A handkerchief.

HOW IT WORKS — Tie a single knot in the rope midway between the center of the rope and the left end. Pull the knot smaller but not too tight. The spectator is unaware of this bit of preparation.

Introduce the rope and hold the knotted portion hidden in your left hand. Let the rest of the rope hang down. Display the cutter in your right hand, then thread one of its handle openings through the hanging end.

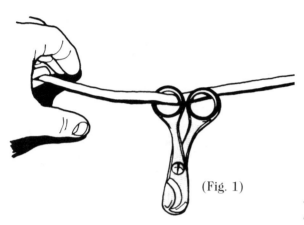

Ask two spectators to assist and have each one hold an end. Your left hand continues holding the part of the rope with the knot, keeping the knot concealed. (Fig. 1) Hold the right side of the rope in a similar manner with your right hand. The cutter should hang in between your hands. Slide the cutter back and forth and say, *"The cutter is securely on the rope. Please hold the ends tightly. Do not let go."*

(Fig. 1)

Have someone cover the cutter and your hands with the handkerchief. Under cover of the cloth, open up the secret knot and work it toward the center. Now all you need to do is push the cutter through the loop and into the knot so that it hangs down. (Fig. 2)

Whisk the handkerchief away and let the puzzling aftermath fully register.

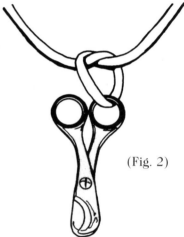

(Fig. 2)

NOT!

You will fool yourself with this bit of hocus-pocus.

WHAT YOU SEE   A single overhand knot is tied into a cord, which is held between your hands. A cigar cutter is held in one hand and is tossed toward the knot. It not only penetrates the rope, it lands in the middle of the knot.

(1) A scissors-type cigar cutter. (2) A two-foot length of cord.

Either tie the overhand knot in the rope prior to performance or tie it in front of your victim. Contrive to secretly insert the right end of the rope through the opening in the handle of the cutter. If you do it beforehand, this eliminates the dexterity factor. Your right hand holds its end of the rope and the cutter, with its blades pointing down. Figure 1 shows the set up without hands showing.

s you hold the ends and display the knot at the center, say: *"Here is a neat mpossibility!"* Continue to hold onto the ends of the rope, but toss the cutter to he left and through the center of the knot. (Fig. 1)

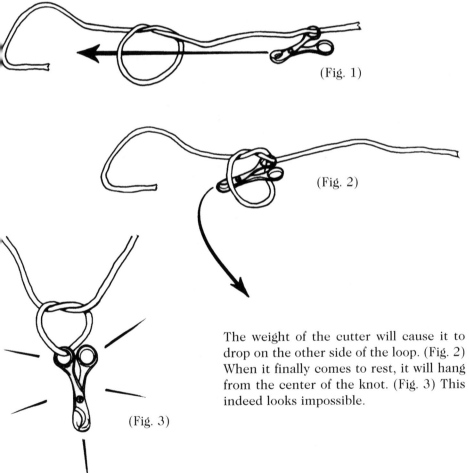

(Fig. 1)

(Fig. 2)

The weight of the cutter will cause it to drop on the other side of the loop. (Fig. 2) When it finally comes to rest, it will hang from the center of the knot. (Fig. 3) This indeed looks impossible.

(Fig. 3)

HOOKED UP

This is one of those puzzling feats that looks remarkably simple until you try to duplicate it. It was shown to us by an old wizard from New Orleans named Eddie Adams.

WHAT YOU SEE — You hook the openings of your cigar cutter onto your pinkies so that the cutting blades are pointing *down*. Your hands are palms up. With a quick, simultaneous turning of both hands, the cutting blades, still hooked to your pinkies, are pointing *up*.

WHAT YOU NEED — A scissors-type cigar cutter.

HOW IT WORKS — Hold your hands palms up with your pinkies side-by-side. Have someone hook the openings of your cutter's handles onto your pinkies so that the cutting blades are pointing toward the floor. (Fig.1)

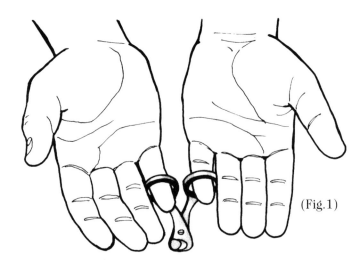

(Fig.1)

Point out that your hands are palms up and that the cutting blade is pointing toward the floor. Say, *"Watch closely. Watch everything I do...because you will be asked to duplicate this simple action."* The next sequence will seem a little tricky. In reality, if you follow the directions exactly, you will have no trouble.

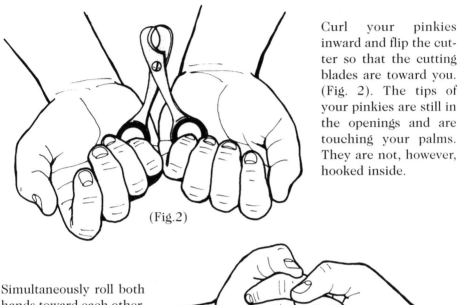

Curl your pinkies inward and flip the cutter so that the cutting blades are toward you. (Fig. 2). The tips of your pinkies are still in the openings and are touching your palms. They are not, however, hooked inside.

(Fig.2)

Simultaneously roll both hands toward each other. Your right hand moves counter-clockwise, your left hand moves clockwise. The *knuckles* of both hands roll against each other. (Fig. 3)

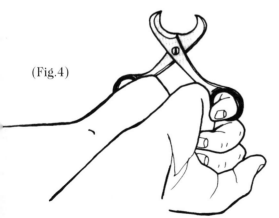

(Fig.3)

(Fig.4)

Meanwhile both hands are also turning inward toward yourself and palms down. Correctly executed, the cutter blades will be pointing *upward*. (Fig.4)

When most people try to duplicate this stunt, they simulate the turnover of the hands but fail to execute the preliminary flip of the cutter. When this happens, the cutter blade will end up pointing down.

ASHES TO ASHES

YOU DO VOODOO

Be prepared to start a religion.

WHAT YOU SEE You ask someone to close one of her hands into a fist as you talk about the powers of voodoo. You take some of your cigar ash and place it on the back of your spectator's fist. Then you slowly rub it into the flesh until most of it disappears. You ask, *"How did that feel?"* Finally, you ask the spectator to open her hand. When she does, she discovers that the ash has apparently penetrated her hand and is now on her palm!

WHAT YOU NEED (1) Cigar ash. (2) A dash of boldness.

HOW IT WORKS This is pure showmanship. Considering the meager requirements of the secret "dirty work," the payoff is disproportionately remarkable. Pay close attention to the underlying psychology and the details of the presentation.

When nobody is looking or paying attention, place the tip of your right second finger into a nearby ashtray that is filled with cigar ashes. You now have a small quantity of ash residue on this finger. As long as you do not touch this finger against anything, the residue will remain there.

Bring up the subject of voodoo and ask if anyone has visited Haiti, New Orleans, or any of the places where voodoo is practiced. Regardless, invite them to participate. Females are much better subjects because they are less guarded and more willing to express their emotions.

When you have a willing participant, position her in front of you so that you are both face-to-face. Place both hands palms down about waist high and say, *"Place your hands like this."* As you utter this instruction, look directly into her eyes, then look down at her hands. The next step is important because you will inconspicuously transfer ash residue from your fingertip to the palm of her left hand. Although this is done in full view, it will not be remembered or considered important. Why? Because it occurs during a ruse.

A ruse in magic parlance is an open, logical, natural action that conceals an important, secret action. Such ruses, if they are cleverly positioned, are almost invisible because they seem spontaneous and not calculated. This is how it works in this case.

As soon as you look down at her hands, simultaneously grab both hands—one with each palm-down hand—so that the tip of your right and left second fingers contact the centers of her palms. (Fig. 1) Simultaneously press your second fingers as you move her hands apart and say, *"Separate your hands a bit and close your hands into fists!"* The spectator will obey your instruction and concentrate on carrying it out. Touching her is excused as being merely demonstrative. You are showing her what to do. Needless to say, during that momentary contact, you have transferred ash residue to her left palm.

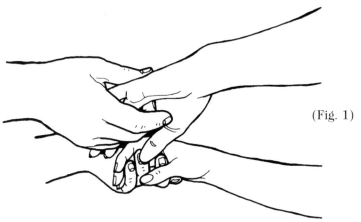

(Fig. 1)

Step back and relax. Directly gaze into her eyes again and hold your left hand near her right fist and make an "opening" gesture as you simultaneously say, *"Open a fist!"* Nine times out of ten, the spectator will open her right hand because of the proximity of *your* left-hand gesture and because most people are right-handed. If she does open her right hand, immediately add: *"Keep your other hand in a tight fist!"*

If she happens to open her left hand, quickly add: *"The one you choose is the one we'll use!"* Ask her to close that hand into a tight fist. In either instance, you have given her the impression that she has chosen one of her hands. In reality, you have induced her to use the correct one! You are now set to perform a minor miracle.

Continue to talk about voodoo, then begin to look around the room for an impromptu ingredient. Say, *"Does anyone have a rooster or some chicken bones or the cremated remains of a one-eyed leper named Lucky?"* Pretend to suddenly spy the ashtray and say, *"Perhaps the remains in this ashtray will do?"* This should seem wholly impromptu.

Place the tip of your right second finger into the ashtray and get more ashes. Needless to say, you are now covering your tracks. The new ash residue covers the old residue. Hold the ash residue for everyone to see, then ask: *"Anyone you know?"*

Continue: *"I'm going to rub some of this ash on your fist!"* Place your right second fingertip against the back of the spectator's chosen fist and rub the ashes against the flesh in tiny circles. Ask, *"Have you ever heard of osmosis, penetration, and minamanipotence?"* Regardless of the answer, add: *"Well, you are about to see what it does!"*

Step back and ask, *"Did you feel anything?"* Finally, ask the spectator to turn her hand palm up and open her fist. When she does, watch her reaction as she sees ashes in her palm. It's a beautiful thing.

TELLTALE ASHES

Edgar Allen Poe would have loved this.

WHAT YOU SEE	Somebody is playing solitaire or a hot game of poker is just breaking up and you ask for the deck of cards, saying: *"This looks like a soothsayer's deck! Are all the cards here?"* You have someone select a card and it is replaced into the deck. The cards are shuffled and placed aside. You place your fingers into a nearby ashtray and pick up some cigar ashes. You roll up your left sleeve and expose your naked forearm.

"See that?" you say. *"You think Popeye had forearms? Watch this!"* You ask the spectator to name his selection. Suppose it is the Seven of Hearts. You rub the ashes against your forearm and the ashes mysteriously form 7H on your skin. |
| **WHAT YOU NEED** | (1) A deck of cards. (2) A bar of *slightly* moist soap. (3) Cigar ashes. |
| **HOW IT WORKS** | Prior to performance decide on a card from the deck—say, the Seven of Hearts. Using a sharp end of the moist soap, write the initials of the Seven of Hearts as 7H on the inside of your forearm and let it dry. (Fig. 1) Where your forearm is marked, it will be a bit filmy; however, otherwise it looks normal and the initials cannot seen. |

After you have asked about the deck and get it into your possession, ask, *"Is this a full deck?"* Spread the cards face up between your hands and quickly locate the Seven of Hearts. Cut the deck at that point so that the Seven of Hearts becomes the top card of the deck. Say, *"I'm going to deal some cards face up on the table..."*

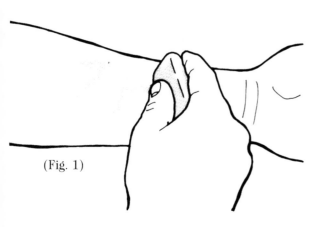

(Fig. 1)

Hold the deck face up in your left hand and start dealing cards face up onto the table. Ask the spectator to say stop whenever he or she likes. When you are stopped, point to the last card dealt with your right forefinger as your left hand simultaneously turns palm down and places the rest of the deck on the table. Say, *"Is there a reason you stopped me on this card?"*

The purpose of this rhetorical question is to direct attention away from the action of your left hand. Pick up the dealt cards and spread them face up between your hands and say, *"You could have stopped on any of these cards..."* Close the spread and place this packet face up in your left hand, which immediately turns palm down and holds the packet above the tabled deck. The reason for this positioning is to present a logical picture for the next discrepant action.

Say, *"But take the next card...which is face down so that I cannot see its identity!"* Take the top card (Seven of Hearts) off the deck with your right hand and place it in front of the spectator. You have now caused him to take the necessary card, even though he thinks his choice was random. Clever, no?

Ask him to look at the card and show it to everyone else. Have him replace it in the deck and shuffle the cards. The rest is showmanship.

Roll up your left sleeve to expose your forearm and say, *"Didn't I say this is a sooth-sayer's deck?"* Take some cigar ashes out of the nearby tray with your right thumb and fingers. Say, *"These ashes will divine your card."* Rub the ashes back and forth over your forearm. Residue will adhere to the filmy initials and they will become visible. (Fig. 2) You will be pleased with the reaction this simple trick evokes.

(Fig. 2)

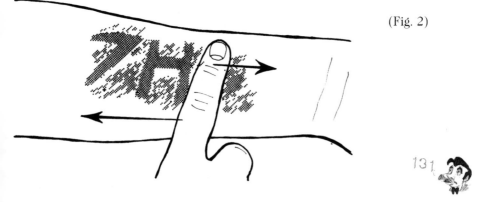

BUSINESS CARD PSYCHIC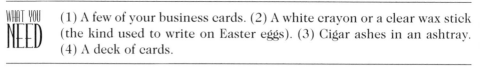

This is a Wall Street version of "Telltale Ashes."

WHAT YOU SEE You show the blank side of your business card. Then a spectator selects a playing card in a random fashion. Some ashes are rubbed across the business card and the initials of the selected card forms out of the ashes.

WHAT YOU NEED (1) A few of your business cards. (2) A white crayon or a clear wax stick (the kind used to write on Easter eggs). (3) Cigar ashes in an ashtray. (4) A deck of cards.

HOW IT WORKS Decide on which card you are going to use. Suppose it is the Jack of Diamonds. Place it tenth from the top of the deck. Take the wax stick and write JD in large letters on the blank side of a business card. Place it among a few other business cards.

Introduce your business cards and show someone an unprepared one. Locate and toss the prepared card on the table with the printed side uppermost. Ask, *"Have you ever heard of reading the runes?"* Regardless of the reply, add: *"Let me show you something using the residue of a cigar."* Show the ashes in the ashtray.

Introduce the deck and show the mixture of cards. Say, *"Instead of having you select a card or permitting you to exercise your free will, we are going to end up with a card by random means."* Hand the deck to your victim and tell him to hold it face down in a dealing position.

Say, *"Give me a number between ten and twenty."* Suppose your victim chooses 14. Ask him to deal fourteen cards face down to the table. Continue: *"Pick up those cards and replace them onto the deck."*

Indicate that two digits make up the chosen number and say, *"Fourteen consists of the numbers one and four. Deal one card onto the table, then deal four more cards."* Believe it or not, the top card of the dealt portion (5 cards) will be the Jack of Diamonds. It will *always* be the card previously chosen (by you) regardless of which number between 10 and 20 is chosen. Have the spectator note this "randomly" chosen card, then replace it, assemble the deck, and shuffle the cards.

Pick up your prepared business card and casually show its blank side. Say, *"Concentrate on the name of your card."* Take a pinch of cigar ash from the ashtray and sprinkle it onto the surface of the business card. Say a few incantations, then rub the ashes across the card. The same principle used in "Telltale Ashes" is applied here. The initials JD will appear on the card as though written in ash.

NICE ASH

Legend has it that the famous trial lawyer, Clarence Darrow, used this device to keep members of the jury riveted as his opponents delivered their arguments and other orations. He was a cigar smoker and as the ash kept getting longer and longer without falling, everyone in the courtroom stared at the end of his cigar...waiting...anticipating when it was finally going to drop. It never did. Needless to say, the jurors had a difficult time concentrating on what the prosecuting attorney was saying. Instead, all they could focus on was Darrow's "Nice Ash."

WHAT YOU SEE	You are smoking your cigar, but you never flick off any ash. After awhile, the length of the ash at the end of your cigar is about three inches long and does not fall off.
WHAT YOU NEED	(1) A hairpin or paper clip, which is straightened out. (2) A cigar.
HOW IT WORKS	Insert the long wire into the head of the cigar. This secret core in the middle prevents a precariously long ash from falling. Light the cigar and begin smoking as usual. After awhile, people will gaze at the long ash, waiting for it to fall. Even if you do not point out the long ash, people with eventually notice it. The longer it gets and the longer you remain silent serves to strengthen this unusual bit of business.

AMAZING CIGAR QUOTE

"By the cigars they smoke, ye shall know the texture of men's souls."

—*John Galsworthy*

CIGAR BOX JUGGLING

"Can anybody juggle cigars?"

"Maybe," said Giovanni, leaping to his feet, *"but they can definitely juggle these!"* He held three cigar boxes between his hands, grinning and puffing on his cigar, no handed. *"This is my ten-minute aerobic exercise!"*

Racherbaumer did not budge, but rolled his eyes. *"Ah, yes! It all stems from the Latin word joculare, meaning—"*

"To jest," interrupted Giovanni. *"It pays to watch the Discovery channel! I can move these boxes just like old W.C.!"*

Cigar box juggling is associated with W.C. Fields, who was long associated with juggling and comedy. In the great days of vaudeville, Fields was a tramp juggler. It is not generally known that Fields hung out at his father's poolroom in Philadelphia. After a fight with his father, he left and lived in an empty boiler room in a vacant lot. Boys in the neighborhood brought him food. It was there that he learned to juggle, using wooden balls and empty cigar boxes.

WHAT YOU NEED   Three cigar boxes with the covers either nailed shut or taped around the ends. Since the ends of the boxes play a big part in the stunts, you can roughen the ends and make them more frictional by gluing sandpaper to them.

AMAZING HINTS

As with anything that takes skill, juggling requires much practice. However, there are hints that will help the beginner develop mastery. Keep in mind that juggling boxes is not tossing them into the air and then catching them nor does it consist of airborne patterns. Since the center box more or less remains in front of your body, only your two hands move, mostly up and down. Your body also moves *up and down*. Therefore, concentrate on the vertical axis.

Think of the two outside or end boxes as being part of your hands. Although your hands hold their respective boxes and your thumbs and fingers are occupied, imagine that the boxes are rectangular *extensions* of your hands. The center box is loose and is the one usually maneuvered.

In many maneuvers, you will begin with all three boxes about waist level. You bend your knees slightly, then move your body upward and your arms and hands upward to about chest level. You execute the maneuver on the upward movement and the action is completed as everything moves down to your original position again.

BEGINNING

Stack the three boxes on end. Bend over and place your left hand on the long side of the bottom box and your right hand on the long side of the top box. Press the two outside boxes together, then turn them *horizontally* and hold them together with both hands at waist-level. Your hands are palm down and hold the now top sides of the outside boxes. (Fig. 1) This is a starting position.

(Fig. 1)

TAKE OUT

Hold the boxes at waist-level or the starting position. Move them upward and separate the outside boxes a bit so that the center box is momentarily disengaged and airborne, yet all three boxes are more or less aligned on the horizontal axis.

The next action is tricky and quick. Move your palm-down right hand to the top-side of the center box after it separates from the outside box. (Fig. 1) Grab the center box and move it to the right of the original right-hand box. This is done at the top of the upward movement. As gravity comes into play and the "loose" box is moving back down, the other two boxes must move together to "trap" the box now between them.

(Fig. 1)

END TURNING

Hold the three boxes in the starting position with your hands palm down and holding the top sides.

Move your hands upward then separate them slightly and simultaneously turn both hands so that their palms face each other. This will turn the end moves to a vertical position, whereupon they come back together and "trap" the center box. (Fig. 1)

(Fig. 1)

If you want to try a fancy finale, move your hands upward and separate them slightly to separate the end boxes from the center one. Use the outer left corner of the right-hand boxes to strike the end of the (horizontal) center box, knocking it upright so that it is aligned with the two outside boxes. Bring the outside boxes together to "trap" the center one.

BOX BALANCING

Stack nine cigar boxes in a even pile in front of you on the floor. Pick the pile up with one hand and transfer it to your other hand while keeping the stack parallel with the floor. When you are holding the stack between your hands, place it on a table on its side with the long sides up and in front of you.

Push the center box forward about three inches, then place each hand on its respective end boxes about midpoint. Press your hands tightly together, then lift the boxes upward to nose-level.

Keep the boxes together by steady pressure, then mesh them together a side at a time, alternating each side. (Fig. 1) The ends of the boxes will press against the center of the box preceding it in a hinge-like way.

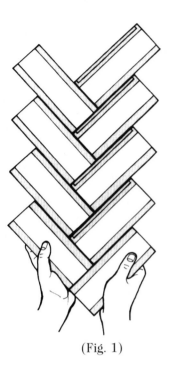

(Fig. 1)

When all the boxes are interlocked in a V-shape, riding upward with five on your right and four on your left, both hands must be simultaneously moved. The left-hand box moves under the right-hand box and both are stacked end to end. (Fig. 2)

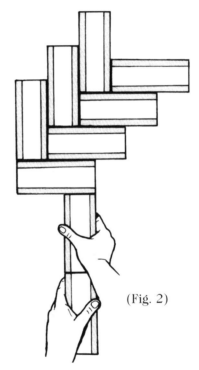

(Fig. 2)

As this occurs, the other interlocked boxes must move to the right with each pair in an L-shape, stacked one on top of the other. The two stacked, vertical boxes balance these seven boxes. Needless to say, finding and maintaining the center of balance is critical.

The final action is to place the lowermost box on your chin. First, tilt your head backwards, then place the lowermost box on your chin. When everything seems to be correctly balanced, let go with your hands, keep your eyes on the stack, and make whatever equilibrium adjustments necessary to maintain a balanced stack.

AMAZING CIGAR
FACTOIDS

According to the *Guinness Book of World Records*, Bruce Block balanced 213 unmodified cigar boxes on his chin for 9.2 seconds on November 5, 1990.

In the last 100 years, there have been 500 billion cigars made and almost all of them have been sold in boxes. There have been over 2 million different brands of cigars in that same period.

The cigar box got its start in 1830 when H. Upmann, the British banking firm, had cigars shipped to London for each of its directors in cedar boxes marked with the firm's logo.

Tony Hyman of Elmira, New York, has an entire room in his house devoted to a collection of 4,000 cigar boxes. He collects cigar boxes that are three-dimensional sculpture, including boxes shaped like beer steins, bottles, mailboxes, log cabins, and made of inlaid wood, serpentine, pressed glass, and other unusual materials.

146

SOLUTIONS

OLIVE FOIL

Take the upright match on the left (forming a side of the glass) and reposition it on the right and parallel to the "stem" match. All that remains—and this is a killer maneuver!—*is* to *slide* the horizontal match originally forming the bottom of the glass to the *right*.

The glass is now upside-down and the olive is outside of it. Is this brilliant, or what?

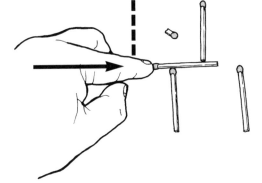

SQUARES GONE

Move matches A, B, and C to form the sides of the new square at the upper right corner.

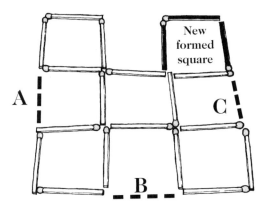

New formed square

A

B

C

141

FIVE TO FOUR

Move matches A and B to form a square. You now have four squares that are staggered.

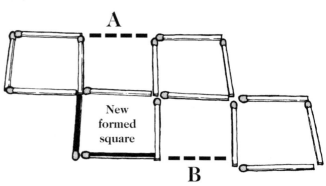

New formed square

MENSA BASH

If you solved the two previous puzzles you will tend to conceptualize in the ways needed to solve those puzzles. This one is much tougher because the initial configuration of a smaller square *within* a larger square induces you to imagine *isolated squares*, not two lareger squares that *overlap* at their corners to form a smaller square. This, coupled with the condition of removing *only four matches*, really messes your mind. Look at the drawing and you will easily see which four matches to reposition.

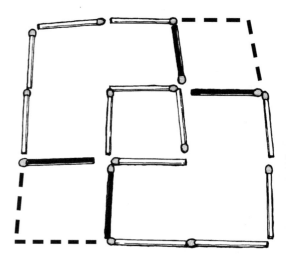

TRIANGULATION

Move and re-position matches A and B to the top.

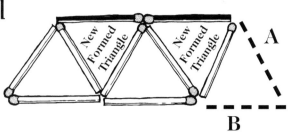

TRIANGULATION OUTDONE

Lateral thinkers may solve this one, but if anyone tries to solve it in a two-dimensional plane, they are doomed. Hold the three matches of the second triangle as shown and you will form four equilateral triangles.

MAKE IT EQUAL

This is a sweet cheat. Place the matches in this equation on a placemat or handkerchief. To make the equation equal, simply turn the placemat upside down.

143

STARLET

Release a drop of water (use a straw) onto the center where the matches are broken. The wood will expand and form a star-shape.

ROOT OF IT

Move and reposition one match to form the square-root sign. Of course, the square root of one equals one.

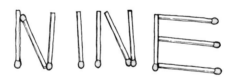

NINNEY

Move the five matches to form four letters spelling out N-I-N-E.

NINE

EDGY

This is another brash cheat. Simply bend the paper match and drop it. It will land on its side or on "edge."

NIM

This is the winning strategy.

Regardless of who begins the game, make certain that one of the following combinations of matches—in any sequence—are in the top, middle, and bottom rows at some stage: 6-4-2 or 5-4-1 or 3-2-1 or 1-1-1 or, when only two rows remain, there must be an identical number of matches (higher than one) in each row. You can generally reach this stage after two or three turns.

Sample game:

Suppose your opponent takes away one match from the top row, leaving two. Your next move would be to remove only one match from the third row. This leaves a 2-5-6 combination.

Suppose your opponent takes three matches from the bottom row on his next move. That leaves 2-5-3. You need to take out four matches from the center row to obtain a 2-1-3 combination, which is one of the required winning combinations (remember: *sequence* is not important. 2-1-3 is the same as 3-2-1.)

Suppose your opponent takes two matches from the bottom row, leaving 2-1-1. His fate is now sealed. Simply take one match from the top row, leaving 1-1-1. He can only take one of the three remaining matches. You take one of the remaining two and your opponent loses.

ABOUT FACE FISH

Move match A to form the tri-angular-shaped body, then move match B to formt the rear fin as shown. The "fish" is upside down swimming in the opposite direction.

FLYING SOUTH

This is like "About-Face Fish" except that a "flock" flies in the opposite direction. Move match A to the bottom to become the lead-bird "flying south." Then move matches B and C from the left and right end of the row of four to the left side of the row of three. Now the "birds" are "flying south" in formation.

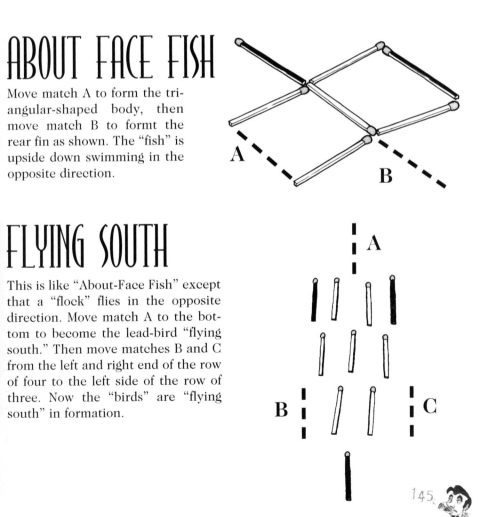

145.

PERFECT SQUARE

This is a bit of a cheat, but it satisfies the conditions. Slide the match on the right a fraction to form a tiny square (space) in the center. Take the money and run.

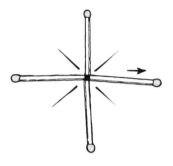

GORDIAN NIGHTMARE

Take the smaller end loop that forms the Bridle Hitch (marked X) and pull it through opening A so that it runs *under* the two strands which are also threaded through the *same* opening. Then work it further down and *over* the downward blades, hence the *entire* cutter. Now the loop wil slip free. Follow the arrows.

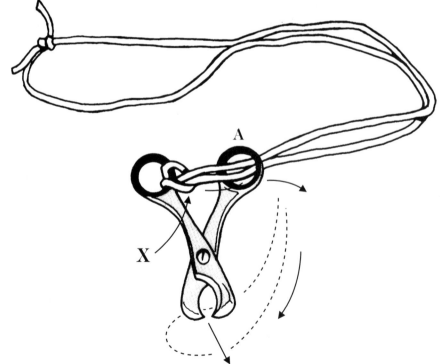

Devin Crane

To order additional copies of

THE AMAZING CIGAR,

to find out about our other publications,

or to get information about hiring the ultimate magic and cigar

entertainers for corporate events

Contact:

Magic Marketing Concepts, Inc.

(407) 657-7655

or visit our website:
www.wowmom.com